Contents

Sanatana Dharma

Form to Reach the Formless   7

Devotion Based on Fear to Devotion
Based on Love   10

Idol Worship   13

Is Spirituality Escapism?   17

Is the World an Illusion?   20

The Importance of the Guru   24

How to Pray   28

Reincarnation   31

Is God Partial?   34

The Essence of Spirituality

Death Is Not the End   38

Supreme Bliss Here and Now   43

Religion & Spirituality   47

The Creator & The Creation   51

The Essence of All Religions   54

Loving Yourself   57

Family Life
Don't Trap Your Love Inside   60

Culture in Education   63

Raising Children in the Modern World   67

Harmonious Relationships   71

Trust Is the Foundation of Strong Relationships   74

Religious Festivals and Texts
The Devotion in the Ramayana   78

Imbibe the Essence of Religious Festivals   82

Navaratri Should Teach Us Humility   86

On Christmas Give the Gift of Love   89

Sivaratri Is for Immersing Ourselves in God   92

The Eternal Beauty That We Are

A Collection of Timeless Messages from Amma

Compiled and Translated by
Swami Amritaswarupananda Puri

Mata Amritanandamayi Center, San Ramon
California, United States

The Eternal Beauty That We Are
A Collection of Timeless Messages from Amma

Compiled and Translated by
Swami Amritaswarupananda Puri

Published By:
Mata Amritanandamayi Center
P.O. Box 613
San Ramon, CA 94583-0613, USA

First printing: October 2019

In India:
www.amritapuri.org
inform@amritapuri.org

In Europe:
www.amma-europe.org

In US:
www.amma.org

To Worship Krishna Is to Become
Krishna   95

Love

Climb the Ladder of Love to Its Peak   98

Love Makes Our Life Divine   101

The Nature of the Guru

For the Subtlest Science,
a Teacher Is Needed   104

Mahatmas Come Down to Raise Us Up
                                        109

The Guru Is the Ultimate Truth
Embodied   112

Our Culture

Respecting Our Elders   116

Restoring the Harmony of Nature   119

Welcome All "Unexpected Guests"   123

A Light in This Darkness   126

Spiritual Practices & Vedic Science

Samadhi   129

Yoga Versus Physical Exercise   133

Astrology & Faith in God   136

Values

Avoid Preconceptions   141

Awaken Awareness   145

Bad Habits   148

Devotion Is an End in Itself   151

Action & Thought   154

Don't Fall Slave to Anger   157

Enthusiasm Is the Secret to Success   161

Healing From Guilt Over Past Mistakes
                                           164

In Our Rush, Beauty Is Lost   167

Learn to Give Back to Society   170

Overcoming Tension   173

Simple Living and Self-Sacrifice   175

Sympathy Versus Compassion   178

The Correct Attitude Is Everything   181

The Path to Peace   184

Keep the Attitude of a Beginner   188

Sanatana Dharma

Form to Reach the Formless

Children, the sole cause for the creation, sustenance and destruction of the universe is God. Here, those who believe in God will all agree. However, believers will have varied opinions and doubts regarding God's true nature: What is the real name and form of God? What are His attributes?

In truth, God can neither be understood with the intellect nor explained with mere words. Regardless, through spiritual practices we can experience and realise God. That experience is indescribable. When a baby gets hurt, can it explain, "It hurts this much"? Or when it is happy, can it explain that "I am this happy"?

Just as water can manifest as ice, liquid or steam, God is both with and without attributes. He manifests as duality and as the multifaceted universe.

God doesn't have a particular name or form but is instead like an actor appearing on the stage, playing various roles. In this way, according to the devotee's desire, God assumes different states of being and forms such as Siva, Vishnu and Devi. When heated up, a chocolate figurine will melt and become formless. But regardless of whatever form the chocolate takes, the true nature of the chocolate always remains the same.

To conceptualise and worship God, it is easiest to visualise Him as having a form. One who is thirsty will need to cup his hand or use a vessel in order to get water from a river. A person who has a long stick can knock a mango from a tree, even if he cannot climb. Similarly, conceptualising God as having a form and using that form as our instrument, we can worship and realise God.

Once, a mother bird went searching for food and somehow hurt one of her wings. She was unable to fly and became very sad because she couldn't get back to her nest on the other side of the river. Worrying about her helpless baby birds, she became very anxious. It was then that she saw a chunk of ice floating towards her. Without much difficulty, she jumped onto it. A favourable wind then pushed the ice to the opposite shore, and she was able to get back to her nest.

Those of us struggling in distress to know the formless God without any attribute are just like this injured bird trying to get home. We can realise God by worshipping Him as having form and other attributes. The water in the river had no shape, but it became a solid chunk of ice, allowing the helpless bird to cross the river. Likewise, to attain freedom from the ocean of *samsara*, worshipping God with form and attributes should become a constant companion. Then the favourable breeze of divine grace will lead us to Liberation.

Devotion Based on Fear to Devotion Based on Love

Children, some people ask, "What is the importance of *bhaya bhakti* [devotion with fear] in the path of devotion? Isn't it unhealthy?"

It cannot be said that *bhaya bhakti* is unhealthy. Even though there is no place for fear in the wholeness and perfection of devotion, some fear definitely helps a beginner to grow. God, who is the sole protector of the universe, is also the bestower of the results of actions to all beings. God protects all good people and punishes the wicked. A person who realises that he will have to suffer the consequences of all his bad deeds will feel some fear mixed with his devotion. This fear makes him strong, however, because it awakens his sense of discrimination. It helps him to stop making mistakes and to move forward along the right path.

Bhaya bhakti is not like the fear a slave has towards his master. It is rather like a student feeling fear mixed with respect towards his teacher or like a child showing innocent love towards his mother. This is the attitude we must have towards God.

A child loves his mother. He truly believes that his mother is his sole protector. However, he also knows that if he makes a mistake, his mother will not hesitate to punish him. So, there is definitely a bit of fear mixed in with his love for her. It is this fear that saves him from many accidents and mistakes. A child has a lot of immature tendencies and weaknesses. That often prompts him to commit mistakes. However, due to his fear that his mother will get angry and punish him, he turns away from those mistakes. Thus, his fear towards his mother awakens his sense of discrimination, and he gradually gains the strength to walk along the right path. But the fear never stops him from experiencing his mother's love. On the other hand, it helps him to grow.

At a young age children study well because of the fear that the teacher will punish them if they do not. That fear helps them overcome their laziness and work hard to learn and achieve academic excellence. By the time they reach higher grades, this fear disappears. But by then, they have acquired enough discrimination to earnestly pursue their studies without it. Then there is no need for fear. They only have respect and obedience towards their teachers. An attitude like this towards God is present in most devotees.

As a devotee travels along the path, *bhaya bhakti* transforms into love-filled devotion. In that devotion, there is absolutely no fear. Due to one's love for God, even punishment from God is welcomed with joy and happiness. The intensity of that devotion will annihilate any tendencies to commit a mistake.

A true devotee is like a small child resting in the lap of his loving mother. He forgets everything else.

Idol Worship

Someone recently asked me, "Instead of worshipping the idol, shouldn't we worship the sculptor who created it?"

Children, when we see our nation's flag, do our thoughts go to the tailor who stitched it? No. No one seems to remember him. What we remember is our country. In the same way, when we see an idol, our thoughts shouldn't go to the sculptor but to the principle that the idol represents: the true Creator—the Creator who created this entire universe.

To understand idol worship, one has to understand the principles behind it. In truth, God has no particular name, form or abode. God is beyond time and space. His nature is one of absolute bliss. He is truth without form or any other attribute. However, for most people, worshipping the omnipresent divinity of God without the assistance of a concrete symbol is impossible. Currently, our minds are bound and attached to this material world and its various forms. Idol worship helps turn such minds inwards. There they can gradually come to recognise the divinity that is the mind's substratum.

If we want to see our reflection clearly in a mirror, we first have to wipe away all the dust and grime from the mirror's surface. Similarly, in order to see our true nature in the mirror of the mind, we first have to remove all the impurities currently collected within it. Idol worship gradually purifies our mind and promotes deeper levels of concentration. That is why the ancient sages of Sanatana Dharma stressed the importance of idol worship and temples.

Some say that practicing idol worship indicates an unrefined mind. Only when idol worship is rooted in the misconception that God resides only in one particular place with one particular form can this be said to be true. God is omnipresent. God is the ultimate cause of everything in existence. When we perform idol worship with this understanding, it can never be unrefined; it is a valid means to Self-realisation. If we worship the idol with selfish prayers—prayers only aimed at the fulfilment of our own selfish desires—then it can be called unrefined. But the most unrefined form of idol worship is worshipping the idol while at the same time degrading other people.

When people say "Only worship God; don't worship the devil," it really means that attaining God should be our only goal. The "devil" means desires for money and status that cross *dharma* and other selfish attitudes. It doesn't mean worshipping God through various forms. Idol worship is there wherever symbols and idols are used to awaken the remembrance of God. When we look at it this way, it becomes clear that many people who criticise idol worship actually perform idol worship themselves.

Although God is beyond name and form, we still can worship God in any form we like. In the same house, the father may prefer to worship Lord Siva, the mother Lord Krishna, and the son Devi. This is why it is called *ishta-daivam*—our "favourite deity." We should understand the principles behind worshipping God in various forms. A necklace, a bangle, an earring—all are made of gold. Their substratum is gold. Similarly, the substratum of existence is God. We have to see the unifying substratum of this seemingly diverse world. No matter what be the form of our *ishta-daivam*—Siva, Vishnu, Muruga—we must come to recognise this unity. We must understand that all these forms are but variations of the One. Understanding that people were from different cultures, the ancient sages accepted the invocation of different forms for worshipping God.

Through idol worship, we must achieve the broadmindedness to love and respect all forms of life. By seeing God in the idol and praying to Him, we are purifying our mind and raising ourselves up to a place where we can recognise God in everything. This is the ultimate goal of idol worship.

So many great souls like Sri Ramakrishna Deva, Mirabai, Andal and Kannappa Nayanar attained liberation through idol worship! May my children also awaken to this level of truth.

Is Spirituality Escapism?

Children, people often ask if spirituality isn't just running away from life. You must understand, real spirituality can never be escapism. Running away is the path of cowards. Spirituality is the path of the brave. It is a science that teaches us how to be strong when facing any crisis and how to always maintain happiness and contentment. Spirituality helps us to deeply understand life and to maintain the right attitude towards it.

Spirituality is perceiving your True Self. It is the search into who we are and what the meaning of life is. Through that, we can understand the nature of the world and its objects.

Currently, we believe that happiness lies in material objects. But if that were the case, then why aren't we content upon acquiring them? On the contrary, we see a millionaire owning a jet, a boat and a mansion but still being full of tension and sorrow.

Once, in a village, in two neighbouring huts, lived two families. The head of one of the families saved money and built a good house. Then his neighbour started worrying, "He already owns a house. I'm still living in this hut." So, soon, he started struggling to save money. He also borrowed some. In this way, he strove to build a house. As he did so, he would dream of how one day he would happily live in his new house.

When his house was finally finished, he jumped with joy. He invited his relatives and friends for a feast and started living happily in the new house. But after a few months, he became depressed. Someone asked him, "What's wrong?"

He replied, "Our neighbour has installed air-conditioning in his house and laid a marble floor. My house is a dump."

The house that once filled him with joy was now a source of sorrow. This proves that happiness is not located in material objects. In reality, our experience of happiness is dependent upon our mind. When the mind becomes peaceful, we will experience happiness without any problem.

When we realise the secret behind happiness, we will stop blindly chasing material objects. When we imbibe spirituality, we will be able to see our fellow man as our own Self. We will share our extra money with the poor and needy. We will become ready to love and serve others with an open heart. True spiritual attainment is in having the mental strength to face anything and in compassionately serving the world.

Is the World an Illusion?

Many people ask Amma, "Why is this world referred to as *maya*—an illusion?"

Children, an illusion is something that hides the truth and takes us away from the truth. The world is called an illusion because it can hide the truth—the source of eternal peace—from us. What is our current experience? We believe that various material attainments, relationships and objects will give us eternal peace and happiness, and we pursue them eagerly. In reality, this pursuit leads us away from peace. That is *maya*—illusion.

While dreaming, the dream world is very real to the dreamer. But when he wakes up, he realises none of it was real. Similarly, due to our lack of spiritual understanding, we are now living in a dreamlike world—a state of confusion. Only when we awaken from this ignorance, will we realise what Truth really is.

Once, a very poor youth was sitting on the riverbank fishing. After a while, he saw an elephant approaching him, accompanied by a large crowd of people. The elephant was holding a flower garland in its trunk. It stopped before him and placed the garland around his neck. The crowd enthusiastically applauded. The people told him that this was the ritual for choosing the next king. Whoever the elephant chose to garland would become the next king. Soon, the youth was consecrated the king and married the princess.

One day, both the princess and the youth were riding horses atop a mountain near the palace. Suddenly, there was a big storm. Both horses and riders fell off the mountain. The princess and the horses plummeted to their death, but somehow, as he was falling, the youth managed to grab hold of a tree branch and survive. It was a long way down, but he had no other choice. He had to let go. He closed his eyes and dropped.

When he opened them, he did not see the mountain or the horses or his princess. He only saw the riverbank and his fishing pole. Then he realised that he had fallen asleep and it all had been a dream.

Regardless of how real it all seemed when he was dreaming, the boy was not at all sad about losing his princess or his palace.

Today, just like the boy in the story, we live in a dream world, totally ignorant about reality. In this dream world, most people are very attached to success and profit and fear failure and loss. When things do not work out in their favour, they feel their entire world is coming to an end! That world—the world where success equals happiness and failure equals sorrow—is a dream from which we need to awaken. It is *maya*. There is only one source of true happiness, and that is the *atma*—our True Self. We need to wake up to this understanding. Then, no matter what happens in life, we will remain full of peace and bliss.

If this world is *maya*, in what way should we approach it? Should we reject it? Definitely not. We only need to approach the world and the various experiences it presents us with *viveka*—discrimination. Then the world itself will help guide us to the Truth. If we can do this, we will be able to see an element of goodness in everything. A murderer uses a knife to kill, but a physician uses it to save lives. So, instead of rejecting the world, saying "It's just an illusion," try to understand the value and principles behind all of your experiences in life. Let that understanding guide you.

The ones who understand the nature of *maya* are the true protectors of the world. They never fall victim to *maya*'s illusion. Those who fail to understand the nature of the world not only destroy themselves, but they also become a burden to others. Those who see goodness in everything are lead to goodness. From there, they realise the Truth.

The Importance of the Guru

Children, some people ask, "If God and *guru* are ultimately within, what is the need for an external *guru*?" It is true that God and *guru* exist within, but most of us lack the capacity to know God within or to imbibe the guidance of the inner *guru*. A rare few are born with a spiritual disposition and tendencies acquired from previous births. Such people may be able to realise the spiritual truth without the help of a living *guru*, but most people need a *guru*.

A *sadguru* is indeed God in human form. The *guru* leads the disciple, who is bound by many weaknesses and vices, with extreme kindness and patience. The *guru* provides the necessary instructions, teachings and clarifications so that we can assimilate the spiritual principles in their simplest and purest form. Thus, for the disciple, the *guru's* place is even above God.

Spirituality is the polar opposite of materialism. Thus, when we come to spiritual life with our materialistic worldview, we fail. It takes us a while to understand. However, the *guru*, in his infinite patience, explains and demonstrates, over and over again, until the disciple gets it right, once and for all. If you want to learn a foreign language, the best way is to live with a native speaker. The *guru* is the native speaker of spirituality.

What the scriptures teach us is very subtle. It is the secret of our true being, explaining it to be the very existence upon which the universe subsides. Enslaved by the mind and countless layers of accumulated tendencies, we have no frame of reference for understanding such truth. Everything the *guru* teaches us is the opposite of what we have ever learned. We've been conditioned to think happiness comes from objects, but the *guru* tells us, "No, happiness only comes from within." We've been told to try to fulfil our desires; the *guru* tells us it's better to transcend them. We've been told we are born and one day will die; the *guru* tells us we are birthless and immortal. So, basically, the *guru's* job is to reshape us completely. The *guru* can be compared to a sculptor. The sculptor sees the sculpture hidden inside the stone. As he chisels away the unnecessary parts of the stone, the hidden beautiful form gradually emerges. Like this, a true *guru* brings out the truth at the core of the disciple. When the disciple follows the *guru's* teachings and does his spiritual practices, his ignorance disappears and truth manifests.

When rain falls on a mountaintop, the water flows downwards. The nature of our mind is similar. One minute we may think our mind is fully exalted and revelling in higher realms. However, within seconds, it sinks down to the bottom. The *guru* knows the weaknesses of the disciple's mind, and he knows how to help him transcend them. Even though the nature of water is to flow downwards, the same water can become steam and ascend in the presence of the sun's heat. The *guru* knows that by kindling awareness in his disciple, the disciple's mind can be raised to higher levels. This is the aim of the *guru*. He constantly strives for this. Once the disciple's awareness and inner *guru* are fully awakened, he will not need the help of the external *guru*.

Any word uttered by such an awakened person is a *satsang*. Any action done by such a person is a prayer, a meditation. Every breath taken by such an individual can only benefit the world.

For the *guru* to appear, disciplehood should first awaken. The individual must be ready to be disciplined. Preparedness is essential in order to acquire any form of knowledge. As far as the *sadguru* is concerned, only one thing exists: an immortal oneness. He ultimately sees everything as pure consciousness. For him, there is neither *guru* nor disciple, neither mother nor child—only eternal unity. However, for our benefit, the *guru* comes down to our level. The disciple's longing to know the reality of his true being is vital.

How to Pray

Children, worship is the greatest way to establish a lasting emotional relationship with God and to open our hearts to God. It is a bridge that connects the individual self to the Supreme Self. A small child comes home from school, drops his slate and pencil, and runs to his mother. He eagerly tells her all that happened at school, the stories his teacher told and about the birds he saw on his way home. Similarly, praying will help us develop a heartfelt connection with God. When we share our burdens with God, it helps us unload them.

We must have the attitude that God is our only solace. We must consider God as our best friend—a friend who will always be with us, in every situation and in any danger. When we open our heart to God, unknowingly we are uplifted to the higher planes of devotion.

However, today, many people do not understand the proper use of prayer. Many think that prayer is just a means to fulfil their own worldly desires. The love of such people is not for God but for material things. In today's world, people even pray that tragedy befalls others.

A true devotee should never even think of harming others. Our prayers should be, "O God! May I not commit any mistakes! Please, give me the strength to forgive other's mistakes! Please, forgive my mistakes and please bless everyone in creation." When we pray like this, we will become peaceful. The vibrations of such prayers purify the atmosphere. When our environment becomes pure, it produces favourable effects in our life as well.

Prayers for the benefit of the world are the highest form of prayer. What is needed are prayers totally devoid of selfish desires. When we pluck flowers for worship, we are the first ones to enjoy their beauty and fragrance—even though that is not our intention. When we pray for the benefit of the world, our hearts become very expansive. Moreover, these prayers help the world as well.

Just as a candle melts to give light to others, a true devotee desires to sacrifice himself to help others. His goal is to cultivate a mind that gives happiness to others, forgetting his own suffering. Such people do not have to wander searching for God; God will come looking for them. God will be with them, like a servant.

Reincarnation

Many ask whether rebirth is a reality. If this birth is true, then why should rebirth not be real? It is incorrect to think that life can be measured with reasoning alone. Life is a mix of reason and mystery.

We should assume that we have lived before and will live hereafter because we are living now. Everything in the universe is cyclical. We can see this regularity in the changing seasons, earth circling the sun, planets revolving and so on. Similarly, it is not wrong to assume that birth and death are also cyclical.

Once, a pair of twins were conversing while in the womb. The sister told the brother, "I believe there is life beyond this."

The brother did not agree to that. "No way. There's no other world beyond this world that we see and experience now. This world of ours is dark and comfortable. We are getting all our needs met through this cord. We should not lose our relationship with it. We do not have to do anything else."

The sister said, "It is my staunch belief that there is a vast world full of life beyond this dark world."

The brother could not accept these arguments even slightly.

The sister said again, "I have one more thing to say. Perhaps you may have difficulty believing it, but I believe that we have a mother who will give birth to us."

"A *mother*? What foolishness are you saying? Neither you or I have ever seen this 'mother.' I can never believe that a mother, whom we have never met, exists."

The sister said, "During certain silent and quiet moments, I can hear this mother sing. I am then able to experience our mother's love and endearment covering and caressing us."

Saints and sages who are knowers of Truth first spread the knowledge of rebirth to the world. We do not fully experience the results of the good and bad actions we do in this lifetime. We will experience that in the following births. The reason for rebirth is to experience the fruits of our actions.

At the time of death, there will be good and bad tendencies in the being that is leaving the body. The being cannot act according to those latent tendencies without a gross body. Hence, after death, life again enters a body suitable for it.

If we cannot remember the lyrics of a song we learnt when we were young, can we say that we never learnt the song? Similarly, if we cannot remember incidents and experiences of a previous life, we cannot say there was no previous life. It may not be possible for ordinary people to have memories from a previous life, but when the mind becomes subtle through meditation, we will be able to know our previous lives.

Is God Partial?

Some children ask Amma whether God dislikes the wicked and likes the virtuous. In reality, God is not partial. God sees everyone equally. The sun shines equally on all beings, sentient and insentient. Saying "God doesn't love me" is like closing the doors and windows of the room and complaining that the sun refuses to give me light. The river gives equal water to both the sandalwood tree and the Indian coral tree growing on its bank. The river is not to blame that the sandal tree is fragrant while the coral tree is thorny. Similarly, God showers grace on everyone equally, but we are able to absorb that grace only according to the nature of our mind.

Most people pray to God because they want something. While the coffin-maker prays, "O God! Make someone die today so that I can sell at least one coffin," a sick man's wife and child pray for their husband and father to get well soon. Which of these prayers should God accept? What befalls them is the results of their own actions. There is no use blaming God for that. God is the dispenser of the results of one's *karma*, but He is never partial.

As per our actions, so are the fruits. If we perform good deeds, we will enjoy happiness. If our actions are bad, we will have to experience sorrow. This rule is the same for everyone. However, some people perform actions with the attitude, "I am not the doer." They surrender all their actions to God and perform their *karma*. Selfishness and ego will be relatively less in them. Such people will be able to receive more of God's grace.

The sun reflects well in clear water, but it reflects hazily in water full of moss. Similarly, a mind covered with arrogance, selfishness and other dirt will find it difficult to feel the grace of God. For that, one's heart should be pure; one should have compassion towards the suffering. Such people do not have to do anything for God's grace to flow to them.

Amma remembers an incident. Many people came to a particular *ashram* to see and obtain the blessings of the *mahatma* who lived there. One day, when he was meeting visitors, a small child suddenly vomited on the floor. The stench was unbearable and some people covered their noses, while others walked around the mess. Some others commented on how unhygienic the *ashram* was and left the place. Some others complained saying, "*Guru*, a child has vomited there. It smells really bad there. You should tell someone to clean the floor." Hearing all this, the *mahatma* got up to clean the floor himself. But when he reached there, he saw a young boy clearing away the vomit and washing the floor with soap and water. Although the place was filled with people, only the young boy had thought to do this. All the others did was complain. The young boy's selfless attitude of joyfully doing something good for others attracted the *mahatma*. The *mahatma's* heart melted. He spontaneously felt compassion and love towards the boy. He thought, "If there were more people in this world with this boy's attitude, this world would become a heaven."

Everyone was equal in the eyes of the *mahatma*. Nevertheless, he felt a special compassion towards this boy. The boy's attitude of cleaning the floor with the same alacrity as he cleaned dirt from his own body made him a fitting vessel to receive the *guru's* grace. God's grace is also like this. God showers His grace on everyone all the time. If we dig a hole on the riverbank, water will flow into it. Similarly, God's grace will flow into a heart that has the qualities of selflessness, compassion and virtue.

God is impartial. He is beyond all differences, has equal vision and is unattached. We should purify our actions and attitude, and have firm faith in God's will. If we have this, we will certainly receive God's grace. We will be able to maintain peace and contentment in happiness as well as sorrow, in gain as well as loss, in success as well as failure.

The Essence of Spirituality

Death Is Not the End

Children, the desire to survive and the fear of death are natural. Humans fear death because, with death, we lose everything we've worked so hard to accumulate. We can overcome this fear, but to do so we must learn to face death while we are living.

Two patients were on their death bed in a hospital. One was a world-famous writer. The other was a 12-year-old girl. The doctors were trying hard to save the life of the writer, but none of their treatments were working. The physical and mental toll of his ordeal reflected in his face. He started to wail, "What will happen to me? I see nothing but darkness!" In his final moments, he was swallowed by fear and loneliness.

The little girl's state was totally different. She also knew death was coming for her. Regardless, she was very cheerful. Her small face radiated with her smile. The doctors and the nurses were surprised. Thinking of the writer's torment, they asked the little girl, "Child, you smile as though you are totally unaware of the fact that you are dying. Are you not afraid of dying?" She innocently answered, "Why should I be afraid of death when my most beloved God is right next to me all the time? I can hear Him calling me, 'My child, come to me.'" A few days later, when she passed away, there was a smile upon her tiny lips.

The writer may have won name and fame, but when death came for him, he was totally crushed. On the other hand, the little girl had established a loving relationship with God. She firmly believed that she was very safe in His hands. Hence, she felt no fear of death at all. If we want to meet death fearlessly with a smile, we should either have the innocent faith of this girl or we must think, "I am not the body, I am the Self. The Self never dies."

Here is a story from the Upanishads: Uddalaka was a great sage. He had a son by the name of

Svetaketu. At 24, after many years studying in his *guru's* hermitage, Svetaketu returned home. He thought he had mastered everything under the sun. Uddalaka immediately sensed his son's false pride and wanted to correct him. One day he called Svetaketu and said, "Son, I think you feel you've mastered every form of knowledge on the face of the earth, but have you learnt that knowledge by which what is unheard is heard, what is not understood is understood, and what is unknown is known?"

"What is that knowledge, father?" Svetaketu asked.

His father replied, "Just as by one lump of clay everything that consists of clay is known, my child, so too it is with that knowledge, knowing which one knows all."

"It could be that my revered teachers were ignorant of that knowledge. Otherwise, they would have imparted it to me. Father, can you please enlighten me?"

"So be it," said Uddalaka. "Bring me a fruit from that yonder banyan tree."

"Here it is, father."

"Cut it open."

"It is done."

"What do you see there?"

"Some seeds, Father, exceedingly small."

"Cut one of those."

"It is cut, Father."

"What do you see there?"

"Nothing at all."

Uddalaka said, "My son, that subtle essence that you cannot perceive—from that has arisen this huge banyan tree. That which is the subtle essence is the bedrock of all existence. Dear boy, that which is the finest essence, the whole universe has That as its soul. You are That, O Svetaketu."

Everything arises out of this so-called "nothingness." That indeed is the mystery of life. One day when the tree, or anything for that matter, disappears, you don't know where it has gone. This is the case with all living beings. We emerge out of the infinity of nothingness. In truth, even while we live in this world, we are a nothing. At the end, we disappear back into this sea of nothingness. However, that nothingness is not a void but pure undivided consciousness, that which the scriptures call *sat-cit-ananda*—pure existence, pure consciousness, pure bliss.

In reality, we come from that totality of consciousness, and we go back to that same totality. That is why great masters say that death, if viewed positively, can be a transforming and beautiful experience. When we view death confined within our small world of limitations, it creates great fear. Conversely, when we view it from the perspective of the totality, it liberates us from all fear, agony and anxiety. It takes us beyond all limitations.

In fact, death is not the end of life. We end each sentence with a period. We do so, so that we can write the next sentence. Death is just like this period mark. Death for those who are born and birth for those who die are preordained. Death is simply a continuation of life. If we place our faith in God and are aware of the truth, we can definitely conquer death and the fear of death.

Supreme Bliss Here and Now

Children, the scriptures say that the ultimate goal of human life is liberation. It is not experiencing heavenly comfort and joy or arriving at the abode of our favourite deity after death. Liberation is supreme bliss here and now. It is freedom from all forms of intellectual and emotional bondage—a state wherein all sorrows disappear and you feel at peace, irrespective of your circumstances.

It is incorrect to think liberation is something that one attains after death. Liberation has to be experienced while living in this world. That is where it is most needed. It is while living here, in this world, while existing in the chaos and confusion of diverse situations—physical, emotional and intellectual—that we should have this most beautiful experience of total independence. That experience is not in running away and escaping from life. Conversely, it is in living life fully, accepting all that it sends our way. The rainbow fills us with beauty and joy only when we accept all its colours equally.

Similarly, life's excitement and beauty lie in seeing its oneness in and through all the contradictions. Behold that oneness everywhere and then act in this world. Thus, spirituality is not life-negating, but life-affirming.

Life is full of pairs of opposites. We cannot imagine a world without comfort and hardship, birth and death, light and darkness. Sorrow arises when we accept only one aspect of life and reject the other. We like to always be healthy, but never want to be ill. We accept life, but reject death. We appreciate and welcome success, but reject failure. Life cannot exist without dual experiences. Accepting life in its totality, seeing all dualities as different faces of the same life phenomenon—the one and only consciousness—is the peak of spiritual realisation. Then alone will we be free from all sorrow and experience unbroken happiness in all situations. If we realise that comfort and hardship are the very nature of life, we will be able to accept them with equanimity.

Once a *sannyasi* lived in a hut in a village. People respected him because of his pure and simple lifestyle. The unmarried daughter of a businessman of that village became pregnant. At first, she wouldn't say who the child's father was. However, her relatives pressured her and finally she said it was the *sannyasi*. After scolding the *sannyasi*, the girl's father said, "Since you have ruined my daughter's reputation, you should bring up the child." Without even the slightest anger or embarrassment, the *sannyasi* said, "Let it be."

As soon as the girl gave birth, the father entrusted the child with the *sannyasi*. The villagers now hated the monk and began regularly insulting him, but he never took it seriously. He just lovingly raised the child. After a year, the girl began to feel repentant. She approached her father and told him that, in fact, the *sannyasi* was not the father; it was a neighbourhood youth. The businessman immediately apologised to the *sannyasi*. "Please forgive me for doubting and insulting you. We will take the child back."

"Let it be so," said the *sannyasi*.

Our true nature is the only source of peace that no problem in this world can disturb.

Those who have realised that truth know that nothing is separate from them. Seeing supreme consciousness in all living and inert beings, they love and serve one and all. They accept any and every circumstance with equanimity.

Life and love are not two; they are one. Without love, there is no life and vice-versa. This fundamental principle, when translated into action, is spirituality. That indeed is self-realisation, or liberation. People all over the world say, "I love you." It seems "love" is trapped between the sense of "I" and "you." Spiritual practices gradually help us to realise "I am love," which is the ultimate truth.

To arrive at this state, we have to understand spirituality and put forth conscious effort. Spirituality is understanding the nature of the mind. It is a science that teaches us how to experience joy and contentment without being restless or getting caught up in the ups and downs of life. This is of foremost importance in life.

Religion & Spirituality

Every faith has two aspects: the religious and the spiritual. Religion is its outer shell; spirituality is the inner essence. Spirituality means awakening to one's true nature. Those who make the effort to know their True Self are the true devotees. Whatever be one's faith, if the core spiritual principles are understood and put into practice, one can attain the ultimate goal of uniting with God. However, if we fail to absorb the spiritual principles, religion will become blind faith, binding us.

The unity of hearts is what brings about religious unity. If that unity is absent, it will be impossible for humanity to come together and work as a team for the collective good. We will only drift apart; our efforts will be fragmented and their results incomplete.

Religion is a pointer, like a signboard. The goal is spiritual experience. For example, pointing to a tree, a person says, "Look at that tree. Do you see the fruit hanging from that branch? If you eat that, you will attain immortality!" If someone were to say this to us, we should climb the tree, pick the fruit and eat it. If, instead, we hold on to the person's finger, we will never enjoy the fruit. This is the same thing that happens when people cling to the scriptural verses, rather than grasping, imbibing and putting into practice the principles to which they point.

Merely reading religious texts without trying to imbibe their principles is like sitting in boat but never using it to row across to the other shore. Just like the boat, the scriptures are a means, not an end in themselves.

Due to our ignorance and limited understanding, we are confining *mahatmas* to the little cages of religion. The words of the *rishis* and *mahatmas* are keys to unlock the treasure of our Self. However, due to misunderstanding, we use those very same keys merely to argue with one another. In this way, we only further inflate our egos and imprison ourselves. If this continues, understanding and interreligious collaboration will forever remain a distant dream.

Once, a renowned artist painted a picture of an enchanting young woman. Whoever saw the painting fell in love with her. Some of them asked the painter if the woman was his beloved. When he said no, each one of them adamantly insisted on marrying her and wouldn't allow anyone else to do so. They demanded, "We want to know where to find this beautiful lady."

The painter told them, "I'm sorry, but actually, I've never seen her. She has no nationality, religion or language. What you see in her is not the beauty of an individual, either. I simply gave eyes, a nose and a form to the beauty I beheld within me."

But none of them believed the painter. They angrily accused him of lying. You just want to make her your own!"

The painter calmly told them, "No, please don't take this painting at surface level. Even if you search all over the world, you won't find her—yet she is the quintessence of all beauty."

Nonetheless, ignoring the words of the painter, the people became infatuated with the paint and the painting. In their intense desire to possess the beautiful woman, they quarrelled and fought with each other and finally perished.

We, too, are like this. Today, we are searching for a God who dwells only in pictures and scriptures. In that search, we have lost our way.

While *mahatmas* give importance to spiritual values, their followers give more importance to institutions. As a result, the very religions meant to spread peace and tranquillity in the world by stringing people together on the thread of love, have become causes of war and conflict. *Mahatmas* are embodiments of spirituality. Their selfless lives are the abode of real religion. Thus, the shortcut to understanding spirituality and how to practice it is to observe *mahatmas*.

The power of all faiths lies in spirituality. Spirituality is the cement that fortifies the edifice of society. Living a so-called "religious life" without assimilating spirituality is like building a tower by simply piling up bricks without using any cement. It will easily crumble. Religion without spirituality is lifeless, like an internal organ cut off from the circulatory system.

The Creator & The Creation

Children, the Creator and the creation are not two, but one—thus says Sanatana Dharma. What is the reason for this? Because nothing is separate from the Creator, and so the Creator and the creation are the same.

There are many examples stated in the scriptures showing the relationship between the Creator and the creation. Even though gold ornaments come in different shapes and sizes, they are all really only gold. No matter how many waves are in the sea, none of them are separate from the ocean. Similarly, God and the universe are not separate but one.

The dance comes from the dancer. Before the dance, during the dance, as well as after the dance, there is only the dancer. Similarly, before creation, during creation, as well as after the creation resolves, there is only God. Everything is God. There is only God. Sanatana Dharma teaches us that there is nothing but God.

A king requested all the artists in his kingdom to make paintings that would express the true beauty of the Himalayas. Numerous artists participated. Each of them painted exquisitely beautiful images. The king and his minister set out to select the best one. It seemed each painting was better than the previous one. Finally, they came to the last. The artist opened his canvas. It was the most beautiful Himalayan mountain. The feeling was like standing next to the real Himalayas. Then—amazingly—the artist started to climb the mountain in his painting. As the king and his entourage watched, the artist ascended to the highest peak. Then the painter disappeared into the painting.

God is like the artist in this story. In his creation of the universe, God is all-pervasive. At the same time, he seems to be invisible. Because we cannot perceive God through our five senses or mind, He remains hidden from us. Even so, because God is our own True Self, we can experience God. Thus, when we realise God within ourselves, we can experience the truth that God and the universe are one.

God is not an individual sitting on a golden throne beyond the skies. God is the all-pervading divinity in all things. If our own finger accidentally pokes our eye, we forgive the finger and soothe the eye. We do this because the finger as well as the eye are not separate from us. Similarly, our *dharma* is to love and serve even the smallest life form with the awareness that God resides in everything. This is the greatest worship of God.

The Essence of All Religions

Children, God lives in our heart. The true nature of God and our own true nature are one and the same. Religions teach us that God created human beings in his own image. Hearing this, many of us may wonder why are we then unable to feel the presence of God and experience true happiness. It is true that God's nature is one and the same with our own. However, due to our ignorance and ego, God—our true nature—has become obscured to us; we are unable to experience it. Instead, we experience sorrow and mental turmoil.

In reality, all religions show us the path to true bliss. However, most of us fail to grasp the real teachings of religion. We have become exclusively fixated on ostentatious rituals and customs. Imagine dozens of jars filled with honey. If we cannot look past the various colours and shapes of the jars, how will we ever taste the sweetness of the honey? This is our current state. Instead of understanding the essence of our religion's teachings, we simply sit stupefied by its superficial aspects.

Once, a man decided to celebrate his 50th birthday in a grand manner. He printed the invitations on fancy, expensive paper. The entire house was painted and decorated. He also bought a beautiful chandelier and hung it in the middle of his banquet room. He decorated the house and its surrounding area. He purchased expensive clothing, a diamond ring and a gold chain, and hired a famous chef to cook an elaborate feast.

Finally, the big day arrived. As the time for the guests to arrive approached, he put on his new clothes, ring and chain, and waited in the banquet hall. The feast was prepared and uniformed servers were standing by. But no one came. As the hour grew later and later, he became more and more restless. "Where is everyone?" That is when he noticed the stack of invitations sitting on his table. In the midst of decorating his house and its surroundings, he had simply forgotten to mail them.

We are a lot like this man. In taking care of our busy lives, we forget to pursue the most important goal of life. Because of this, we are unable to experience true peace and contentment.

Those immersed in the superficial aspects of religion often miss the essence of their religion; they fail to experience the presence of God within. A gardener mowing the lawn sees everything before him only as "grass," but an *ayurvedic* herbalist will see plants of medicinal value hiding in the grass. We must become like the herbalist and realise and assimilate the real values at the heart of our religion—its fundamentals principles.

Children, try to understand the inner essence of your religion and learn the real principles behind its rituals and celebrations. Only through this can you experience the presence of God within you.

Loving Yourself

Children, we are living in a time when people not only hate other people but also themselves. This is why we see a rise in suicides and mentally destructive habits. All religions, spiritual leaders and psychiatrists stress the importance of not only loving others but also loving ourselves.

People generally believe that "loving ourselves" means loving our physical body. Many of us spend a lot of time and money struggling to maintain our physical beauty and health. Upon waking up, many people spend hours in front of the mirror. They go to beauty parlours and gyms. They spend a lot of money and time on such things. Some try to whiten their dark skin or tan their white skin. Some dye their grey hair black. Some dye their black hair red—even green. While taking basic care of one's body and health is important, many of these things are excessive. But does anyone think about the precious time they are wasting? Tragically, no one seems to focus at all on improving their heart and mind.

In a multi-story department store, there were not enough elevators. Hence, the customers had to wait a long time for them to come. Tired of waiting, some customers started to complain and create a commotion. The manager understood that if the problem was not solved quickly, it could affect business. He started trying to think of a solution. Finally, he had an idea. He placed several mirrors around the area where the people had to wait for the elevators. He also had mirrors installed on the walls of the elevators. As soon as he did this, all the complaints stopped. No one felt the time passing as they waited because they were now all totally occupied with looking in the mirror, brushing their hair and applying makeup. They continued this even inside the elevators.

Just as we clean and beautify our body, we should also clean our mind. How do we do this? By quickly removing any negative and harmful thoughts or emotions that enter. Similarly, we must train our intellect to think with discernment.

To do this, we have to gain spiritual knowledge through listening to *satsangs* and spending time with *mahatmas* and other spiritually inclined people. The true meaning of "loving ourselves" is letting the divinity within us shine outwards.

Family Life

Don't Trap Your Love Inside

Children, many women tell me, "When I share the painful feelings in my heart with my husband, he never consoles me. He doesn't even show me a little bit of love." If the husbands are confronted about this, they say, "It's not like that. I love her very much, but all she does is complain." Thus, though they both love each other, neither of them is benefited from that love. They become like two people living on the banks of a river, dying of thirst.

In reality, there is love in everyone. But love that is not expressed is like honey trapped inside a rock. We will not be able to taste its sweetness.

Don't keep your love trapped inside your heart. We must express our love externally through our words and actions. We must love each other with open hearts. We must learn to share our love.

Once a monk visited a jail. There he struck friendship with the prisoners. Among them was a youth. The monk put his hand on the youth's shoulder and lovingly stroked his back. He asked him, "My boy, why did you end up here?"

With tears flowing down his face, the youth said, "In my childhood, if I'd just had someone who would have lovingly placed his hand on my shoulders and talked to me with kindness, I never would have ended up in this prison."

It is extremely important to give love to children, particularly in their early years. In their childhood itself, we must train them to receive and return love to each other.

Love should not be kept hidden in one's heart. It is for sharing through our words, looks and actions. Love is the only wealth that makes a person more happy to give than to receive. It is wealth that we possess but do not see.

So, let us awaken the love that we have inside. Let it be expressed to the world through all our actions, words and gestures. Let us not limit love within the walls of religion, faith or caste. Let us allow it to flow freely everywhere.

May our hearts embrace one another and awaken and share the blissful love inside us. May love embrace all beings and flow. Then our lives will become blessed and divine.

Culture in Education

Children, in the olden days in our country, awareness of the spiritual principles was considered the most important aspect of life. However, today, material knowledge supersedes spirituality in importance. There is no point in trying to turn back the clock. Such efforts will only result in disappointment. What's important now is to learn how to move forward without allowing what remains of our good culture to be destroyed.

A long time ago, children were sent to school only at the age of five. Today, we enroll children in nursery schools when they are even just two and a half years old. Until children turn five, we must show them only love. We shouldn't obstruct their freedom in any way. They must be able to play as they wish. All we have to do is pay attention to their safety—protect them from fire or wandering into ponds. No matter how mischievous they may get, we must only show them love. Even when we point out their wrongdoing, we must do it with extreme love.

Just as they lived protected in their mother's womb for nine months, for the first five years after their birth, they must remain protected in another womb—a womb of love. But, today, this is not the situation.

In the name of education, we put so much of burden on our children—way more than they can carry. At a time when they should be playing with their friends, we have trapped our children in classrooms, like birds in cages. Furthermore, if the children do not get first rank starting with lower kindergarten, the parents become filled with stress. The parents then put even more pressure on their children.

Children live in a world of total innocence. They grow up telling stories to flowers and butterflies. Looking at their world, we have such a feeling of wonder! Their nature is to be happy and spread happiness to others. But instead of imbibing their children's innocence, parents drag their children into their own world—the world of competition and frustration.

Once, two neighbour children were playing, and one child's hands got slightly hurt. Seeing this, his mother scolded the second child's mother. When the argument got out of hand, both the husbands and neighbours started taking sides. Matters escalated. In the midst of all this, someone started looking for the children. When he found them, he saw them happily playing together, having forgotten all about their fight.

These days, parents don't take the time to explain the goal of life to their children or help them learn a lifestyle that leads them to that goal. No one seems to take the time to recognise their child's innate interests and encourage and foster their latent talents. Healthy competition in school can help children improve in their studies and reach their potential, but the level of competition we see today only leads to stress. If they fail to meet their expectations with regard to their exams, they become overwhelmed mentally, and the rest of their life they confront disappointment.

Children, we must think about the purpose of education. It is true that modern education makes it possible to get a degree and land well-paying jobs, but will this give us lasting mental peace? If we are unwilling to inculcate cultural values along with modern education, we will be fostering Ravanas, not Ramas. Awareness of cultural values is the foundation of peace and happiness in our lives. Only through spirituality can we find real culture and supreme wisdom.

Raising Children in the Modern World

Children, this is an age where political corruption, decline in values and abuse of women are on the rise. What is the cause? The world we live in has become like a supermarket; everything and anything is available to anyone and everyone. Thus, so many things attract our mind through so many avenues: the Internet, mobile phones and so on. To keep our balance in these modern times, we need to build a strong foundation based on *dharma* and values. Disciplining the mind in this way must begin from childhood.

Raising our children doesn't just mean scolding and punishing them. We have to lead their minds to goodness. We have to show them the right way, and when they do something good, we have to encourage them to continue. We should not overburden them with studies. They need enough freedom to develop their imagination, independent thinking and to explore their emotions. Along with that, we should show them what is right and wrong, what is *dharma* and what is *adharma*. Things that cannot be taught by scolding and advice can be taught by encouragement and through an example of intelligent behaviour.

There was a boy who used to waste a lot of food. His father tried very lovingly to make him understand that this was wrong. He even scolded him sternly. But nothing worked. Finally, he decided to show him a video. In the beginning of the video, two girls were shown at a restaurant eating chicken. As they ate, they cracked jokes and laughed. When they were full, they dumped their half-eaten meals into the trash. The next scene in the video was of a poor man going through the trash. Seeing two big pieces of chicken the girls had thrown away, he became happy and put them into a small plastic bag. In this way, he slowly filled the plastic bag with the food waste of various people who had eaten at the restaurant. Next, the video followed him back to his village, where he shared all the food he had collected with the children there. The faces of the children shone with happiness. Soon, the food was finished. However, the children were still hungry, so they started licking the insides of the plastic bags. The man's son, who was watching the video, began to cry. He said, "Dad, I will never waste food again."

Establishing the value of discipline in our children is important. It is easy to draw in wet cement. But once it dries, it becomes impossible. Young minds are like wet cement. Therefore, parents need to shower their children with love and affection. They need to inculcate in them values and good culture. Parents should be role models for their children. If we do this, our children will become aware of *dharma* and good habits will naturally grow in them. They will be able to overcome any temptation life may throw their way. They will be able to survive. Our life's goal should not just be to earn money and acquire comfort. We need to nurture an awareness in our children that there are more important goals in life. If we can do this, society will gradually be uplifted, and progress will take place in all areas.

Harmonious Relationships

Children, today we see a lot of marriages in which there isn't any real love. Such marriages are full of conflict and friction. The reason for this is a basic lack of understanding between the husband and wife. In most cases, the couple doesn't even try to understand each other. For a true relationship to develop, a basic understanding of human nature—the nature of men and women—is essential. A man should know what a woman is really like and vice versa. Unfortunately, today this understanding is lacking; they dwell in two isolated worlds with no connection between them. They become like two separate islands with no link between them, not even a ferry service.

Men are mostly intellectual, while women tend to be more emotional. They dwell in two different centres, along two parallel lines. No real meeting takes place. How, then, can there be any love between the two? If the one says "yes," the other will probably say "no." You will rarely hear the harmonious blending of "yes" and "yes" or "no" and "no" in unison. Their different natures should be understood and accepted, and each one, both husband and wife, should make a conscious effort to reach out to the other's feelings, to the heart, and then try to work out their problems with this understanding. They shouldn't try to control each other. They shouldn't say to each other, "I say 'yes,' and therefore you should also say 'yes.'"

Any such attitude should be dropped, for it will only lead to anger—even hatred. The love in such a relationship will be very superficial. If the gulf between these two centres, the intellect and emotions, can be bridged, the sweet music of love will spring forth from within them. This unifying factor is spirituality. If you look at our ancestors, you will see that their marriages were generally more loving than those today. They had much more love and harmony in their lives because they had a better understanding of the spiritual principles and their implications in day-to-day life.

Children, learn to respect each other's feelings. Learn to listen to each other's problems with love and concern. When you listen to your partner, he or she should be able to feel that you are genuinely interested and that you would sincerely like to help. Your partner should feel your care and concern, your respect and admiration. An open acceptance of the other is needed, and there should be no reservations. Still, conflicts are bound to occur; misunderstandings and disagreements may arise. But later, one should be able to say, "I'm sorry, please forgive me. I didn't mean it." Or you could say, "I love you, and I'm deeply concerned about you—don't ever think otherwise. I'm sorry, I shouldn't have said what I said. In my anger I lost my temper and my power of discrimination." Such soothing words will help heal any hurt feelings; they will also contribute to a deep feeling of love between you, even after a big quarrel.

Trust Is the Foundation of Strong Relationships

Children, the foundation of our relationships needs to be mutual trust. The relationship between a husband and wife, between two friends, and between business partners—all are sustainable only if there is mutual trust. In truth, it is our awareness of our own weaknesses that makes us suspect and find faults in others. This results in our inability to enjoy their love. In the end, we also lose our happiness and peace of mind.

When two people begin living together, conflict is only natural. We see this in all relationships. It is human nature to blame all our problems on the other person. Usually, we refuse to take any responsibility ourselves. This attitude is unhealthy, especially for a spiritual seeker. The mere thought, "I'm not an egoistic person, so it's not my fault," itself is already ego.

The ego is very sensitive. What it dislikes most is criticism. Moreover, when our ego becomes unmanageable, it adds to our burden by producing paranoia and fear. This destroys our mental peace and harms our ability to think rationally.

Two children were playing. The boy had some pocket money. The girl had some chocolates. The boy said, "If you give me chocolates, I'll give you money." The girl agreed. She gave him some chocolates. Upon receiving the chocolates, the boy separated the most valuable coins and gave her the less valuable ones. The girl did not realise what was going on, and she laid down and slept peacefully. The boy was still thinking, "I bet she had some really expensive chocolates. Instead of giving them to me, she probably gave me the cheap ones. Just like I set aside the most valuable coins, she must have held back the more expensive chocolates." With all these suspicions, he could not fall asleep.

Some men tell Amma, "I think my wife is having an affair." Some women tell Amma, "I keep watching my husband talking to someone on the phone in a very soft voice. At night, I am unable to sleep at all."

Two people marry craving love, peace and happiness, but due to their suspicious natures, their lives become hell, without any peace. As long as the monster called "suspicion" pervades our mind, no amount of counselling or advice will help. So many families are destroyed like this.

Even though people exchange beautiful and flowery words about their love for each another, somewhere deep down inside, most people believe love is really about taking. In reality, love is about giving. Only through giving love can one grow and help others to grow. If this giving attitude is absent, then the so-called "love" will only cause suffering—both for the lover and for the beloved. We shouldn't think, "Is he a good friend to me?" Rather we should think, "Am I being a good friend to others?"

First, we must be willing to love and trust our spouse. If we are willing to be loving and trustful, 95 percent of that will return to us. Suspicion creates suspicion and trust creates trust. Before finding fault with our partners, we must look inside ourselves. If we have faults, we must correct them.

What often helps is for people in a relationship to speak openly with each other, instead of clinging to suspicions. Don't hesitate to seek the help of friends or even professionals when needed. Being patient with each other, being close, and being there for one another is what makes relationships strong. Above all, understand the spiritual truths and learn to find happiness within. If we can do this, then we will enjoy happiness in relationships as well.

Religious Festivals and Texts

The Devotion in the Ramayana

Children, even after thousands of years, the Ramayana holds a very special place in people's hearts. What is the reason? Because in its pages lies the essence of devotion. The devotion of the Ramayana softens and purifies our heart. Even though the essential nature of bitter gourd is bitter, if we soak it in sugar water for some time, it nevertheless becomes sweet. Similarly, when we bind and surrender our mind to God, all of our mental impurities are removed and our mind becomes pure.

In the Ramayana, we see different forms and expressions of devotion. Bharata's devotion is different from Lakshmana's. Sita's devotion is different from Sabari's. One aspect of devotion is always desiring for closeness and constant companionship of one's beloved. We can see this aspect of devotion in Lakshmana. Lakshmana is forever occupied with serving Lord Rama. To this day, he is remembered as one who constantly renounced food and sleep to serve his Lord. But Bharata's devotion was not like that. His devotion was filled with calmness and gentleness. Seeing himself as Rama's servant, Bharata ruled the country in Rama's absence, as a way to worship Rama.

If one has constant remembrance of God, and complete surrender to God, all one's actions will be worship. On the other hand, without this attitude, even *pujas* and *homas* done at famous temples are mere "jobs," not worship.

The intensity of devotion increases during the absence of our Beloved. This is what we witness both in Sita and the *gopis* of Vrindavan. When Lord Rama was near her, Sita desired the golden deer. She became a slave to her desire. However, after Ravana captured her, Sita's heart was constantly pining for Rama. In that intense sorrow of missing Rama, all of Sita's worldly desires were burnt away. Her heart was purified once more, and she was able to merge with God.

Hanuman's devotion is a combination of qualities such as discrimination, enthusiasm, concentration and intense faith. Once a servant of Sugreeva, after laying his eyes on Lord Rama, Hanuman became totally dedicated to Rama. If the bond Hanuman had with Sugreeva was of worldly nature, what he had with Rama was the bond between the *paramatma* and the *jivatma*—the bond between the Supreme Soul and the individual soul. Hanuman also demonstrates how, through constant chanting of the Lord's name, one can achieve constant remembrance of God.

To gain devotion, one does not need to be born in a higher class or be very knowledgeable. A pure heart is all that is needed. That is what we witness in Sabari. She completely believed her *guru*, who told her that one day Lord Rama would visit her. With the expectation that Rama would come, she cleaned the *ashram* every day and gathered all the materials for worshipping him. She prepared a special place for Rama to sit. In this manner, days, months and years passed. The long wait was not in vain. Lord

Rama came to her hut one day, and he received her loving hospitality. Sabari's story proves that God will come to reside in the hearts of those who wait for Him.

Devotion should not be merely emotional. Devotion based purely on emotion will have intensity, but will be temporary. Hence, devotion founded on knowledge is necessary. Devotion should not be for the fulfilment of our worldly desires. After the seeds of devotion sprout, they should be plucked and planted in the fields of knowledge. When it yields good fruit, then the goal is attained.

Rama was able to awaken the expression of devotion in brothers, friends, subjects—even in birds and other animals. Where there is greatness, we will unknowingly worship it. This is because the seed of devotion is hidden in the heart of each one of us. We should nurture it with our thoughts, words and actions. We should rise in devotion until we see God pervading the entire universe. The Ramayana is a path that takes us to this supreme state.

Imbibe the Essence of Religious Festivals

Children, religious festivals are not traditions to celebrate once a year. We need to imbibe the message at the heart of these festivals and assimilate them into our life. Cultivating devotion and spiritual awareness while continuing to move forward in this material world is an essential principle behind almost all festivals. So too is the need to forgive and forget the wrongs done to you by others. This will help create an atmosphere of freedom, friendliness and unity everywhere, and enable us to open our hearts and help others. Differences such as superior and inferior, employer and employee, master and servant fade into the background.

It has always been India's tradition to connect life, customs, art and knowledge to the worship of God. Just as all the bees follow when the queen bee is caught, similarly if we seek refuge in God, all auspiciousness will come our way. Usually, we depend on God for material gains, but if we can live our lives seeing God in everything and seeing all as His will, we will not only prosper materially but also spiritually. There will be satisfaction and peace in our life. A string of zeroes has no value, but if the number "1" is written before them, suddenly their value becomes huge. Similarly, the one truth that lends value to everything is God: Seeing the world as God.

Many festivals are an expression of the human desire for the future to be better than the present. Today, humankind only seeks external change. But no change made in the external word can ever be permanent. Furthermore, external change often leads to more sorrow than happiness. Hence, while trying to change the external situation, we should also try to change our internal situation. It is not so hard. In reality, it is our actions and our attitude that make this world beautiful or ugly.

One day, God went to visit hell. All the residents of hell started complaining to God. "God, You are very partial. We've had to live in this dirty, smelly hell for ages. Yet, all the while, the residents of heaven have been living in paradise. Is this fair? At least for some time shouldn't we switch places?"

God acquiesced to their prayer. The residents of heaven started living in hell, and the residents of hell started living in heaven. Five to six months thus passed. One day, God paid another visit to hell. What he saw was unbelievable. There were trees and flowers everywhere. The sidewalks and streets were clean. People were singing the praises of God. They were dancing. Everywhere one could only see joy.

Later, God visited the old heaven. It was a painful sight. The fields were now barren, the plants withered. There was not a single flower anywhere. The streets were filled with trash, puddles of urine and piles of human excreta. People were using foul language and constantly getting into fights. In short, the old heaven had become a hell.

Children, this is how life really is. It is we ourselves who create heaven and hell.

We should learn to accept joy and sorrow with equanimity. We should try to cultivate a certain degree of detachment. Neither should we fall apart in the face of difficulty nor should we egoistically dance in joy in times of success. Without an attitude of non-attachment, we will soon become weary. Some people fall so deeply into depression that they even commit suicide. When we give over-importance to material success, life loses its lustre. If we focus more on remembering God and spiritual progress, then the small ups and downs of life will not matter so much. Furthermore, a truly eternal bliss will gradually grow in our hearts.

When we celebrate a festival, we should focus more on imbibing its inner principles than on external celebration. We should imbibe and assimilate these principles in our life. May grace help my children to accomplish this.

Navaratri Should Teach Us Humility

Children, Vijayadasami is a holy day when the members of our youngest generation are led by hand to write the first letters of knowledge. Vijayadasami is also the perfection and wholeness of the worship of Sakti—the divine feminine energy—that occurs throughout the nine days of Navaratri. On that day, children enter the world of knowledge by writing "*hari-sri*" with the blessings of Sarasvati, the goddess of knowledge. The child is able to receive knowledge because it entrusts its forefinger to the hands of the *guru*. The forefinger, which points out the faults and mistakes of others, is a symbol of the ego. By entrusting the forefinger to the *guru*, the child is symbolically surrendering its own ego to the *guru*.

The one who has gained true knowledge will naturally be humble. He will see the good in everyone. He will accept everyone with respect and reverence. The ego alone is our creation;

everything else is the creation of God. It is this ego that we must surrender to God.

On Vijayadasami, both the educated and uneducated mark a new beginning in knowledge by writing *hari-sri* in the same way. Knowledge attains perfection when one, recognising the limitation of the knowledge he has acquired so far, has the humble attitude, "I have much more to know and learn." Then he feels enthusiasm to acquire that new knowledge. Vijayadasami reminds us we should always maintain humility, enthusiasm and an attitude of surrender in life.

On Durgashtami, books, musical instruments and job-related materials are all kept for worship. They are then received back on Vijayadasami. This symbolizes the offering of our very life to God and receiving it back as a blessing of God. Vijayadasami is a symbol of a new beginning in life in a new resolution to remember God.

Whenever we are victorious, we say, "This was my doing!" But when failure comes our way, we say that God is punishing us. It shouldn't be like this. We should have the attitude that God is doing everything—that, "I am merely an instrument in Your hands." Navaratri teaches us that this awareness should awaken within us—that all victories in life are the results of God's blessings and power, and that we should never take personal pride in victory. Remembrance of God and surrendering to God make life blessed.

Navaratri teaches us the importance of step-by-step progress and ultimate liberation through the path of devotion. It teaches us that this is more important than material achievements. By removing the mental impurities of those who make God-realisation their life's aim and by destroying their ego, the Divine Mother awakens our inner spiritual knowledge.

On Christmas Give the Gift of Love

Children, the time of Christmas awakens the vibrations of goodness, compassion and good expectations in people's hearts. Christmas reminds us that our heart must be filled with love for God and for our fellow beings. It reminds us to let go of feelings of selfishness and hatred. *Mahatmas* like Christ demonstrated such goodness through their lives.

Christmas is also the time for healing our relationships with people. Sadly, people often develop negative feelings towards their relatives, friends and colleagues. Most often this occurs when those people have failed to meet our expectations. Negative feelings also arise due to our misunderstandings regarding others as well. In fact, our understanding of others, correct or not, is based on our own culture and experiences. A thief thinks all other people are looking to steal from him!

91

Returning home from work, a woman saw her daughter standing with an apple in each of her hands. She very lovingly said, "My darling daughter, can I have an apple?"

The girl looked at her mother's face and then took a bite from the apple in her right hand. Then, she immediately proceeded to take a bite from the other apple too! Seeing this, the mother's face darkened. She tried to hide it, but she was very disappointed. But, then, the very next moment, her daughter offered the apple in her right hand, saying, "Mom, have this one. It is the sweetest!"

The mother was unable to recognise her own child's innocent love. This story reminds us just how wrong we can be when we judge others based on our own limited understanding.

No matter how experienced or knowledgeable we may be, we must never jump to conclusions and blame or insult others. We must have the good heart to listen to them and understand their side of the story. Even if we think someone has committed the most heinous crime, we must give him an opportunity to explain himself. It is possible that our understanding of the situation is incorrect.

It brings a lot of happiness to everyone to give and receive presents on Christmas. However, the best presents are not the ones you buy in a shop. They are the presents of discarding our bad habits and treating our family, friends and colleagues with love and respect. The true Christmas spirit should shine in all our lives through such positive changes.

Sivaratri Is for Immersing Ourselves in God

Children, temple festivals, celebrations and group worship play an important part in making people turn towards God. When a group of people pray and remember God together, it creates good vibrations in the atmosphere. When a person prays alone, it might be difficult for him to overcome the negative vibrations in the atmosphere. Through group worship, the atmosphere itself becomes favourable for focusing on God. As a result, the culture of spirituality is fortified in people.

The true goal of temple festivals is to create a sturdy foundation for thinking about and worshiping God beyond the few days of the celebrations. One important celebration is Sivaratri. Sivaratri reminds us of the importance of getting rid of negative thoughts and totally immersing ourselves in thoughts of God. It reminds us to strive to attain the most important goal of human birth.

Sivaratri is a festival of renunciation and austerity. Fasting is usually observed during the day, and at night people forgo sleep and sing *bhajans*. Most people are not ready to give up food or sleep. But Sivaratri encourages even lay people to awaken their love for God. It inspires them to forgo food and sleep and spend time meditating and singing *bhajans*.

Once, a *gopika* went to Nandagopa's house to fetch fire to light the evening oil lamp. She was also hoping to see baby Krishna. Upon entering the house, she sharpened the wick of her lamp and started to light it by touching it to the flame of the lamp in the house. Just at that moment, her eyes fell upon baby Krishna in his cradle. Her complete attention turned to Krishna. She became totally oblivious to the fact that her own fingers were beginning to get burnt.

After waiting some time for her daughter to return, the *gopika's* mother went to Nandagopa's house in search of her. The sight she saw was unbelievable. Her daughter was so immersed in the vision of baby Krishna that she was holding the burning wick with her own fingers instead of with the lamp. The *gopika*'s mother ran to her, moving her away from the fire. "What are you doing, my daughter?" she cried. Only then did the *gopika* become aware of the external world. Seeing Krishna, this *gopika* had forgotten everything else. In that exalted state of devoted ecstasy, she did not feel any pain. This story teaches us that if we cultivate love towards superior goals, we will gain strength to overcome all mental and physical weaknesses.

Through the observance of Sivaratri rituals, may we develop love for God and become perfect vessels to receive the grace and blessings of Lord Siva, who is the embodiment of renunciation, austerity and knowledge.

To Worship Krishna Is to Become Krishna

Sri Krishna lived some 5,000 years ago. The fact that people still remember and worship him today is a testament to his greatness. To worship Sri Krishna is to become Sri Krishna. His life should become the model for our lives. Sri Krishna's form is extremely beautiful, but this beauty is not limited to the physical form. It is the undying beauty of the heart.

Moksha—liberation from sorrow—is not something attained after death in some other world. It is something to understand and experience while living here in this world. Sri Krishna taught this principle through the example of his life. Sri Krishna's life story teaches us the meaning of life in this world and how it should be lived. He was a *mahaguru* who celebrated, with gusto, even life's failures. Don't make others cry, but live so that you make them smile—this was the lesson Sri Krishna conveyed through his life. He is the charioteer who leads our chariot towards bliss.

Ordinarily, people like to derive pleasure from the suffering of others. However Sri Krishna's inner bliss was the laughter that overflowed to the world from the fullness of his heart. That was why, even in defeat on the battlefield, his smile never left his face. He reminds us to laugh at our own follies and shortcomings.

Sri Krishna is a role model for all of us, regardless of our chosen field of action. He lived as one with both kings and commoners. Even though born a prince, he tended cattle, drove the chariot, washed the feet of others and even did menial work like clearing away the palm-leaf plates after the feast. He was even ready to go to the unrighteous as a messenger of peace.

He was a revolutionary who raised his voice against improper practices. He discouraged people from offering prayers to Indra for rain, telling them to worship Govardhana Hill instead. He explained to them that, in fact, it was these hills that were responsible for blocking the rainclouds. The first lessons in environmental conservation were imparted to us by Sri Krishna. Even now we must strive to protect Nature and help maintain the harmony in the world around us. When Nature's harmony is disturbed, the relationships between human beings also fall into disharmony.

Most of us become dispirited and lazy if not assigned the kind of work we like. We need to be able to perform all kinds of work with joy and contentment. We should all strive to emulate the enthusiasm and patience demonstrated by Sri Krishna. Sometimes circumstances will be favourable, sometimes unfavourable. Regardless, perform your duties with enthusiasm. You may engage in any and all types of duties, but inwardly remain a witness. This is the meaning of Sri Krishna's smile. This is the principle that is at the heart of Lord Krishna's message to the world.

Love

Climb the Ladder of Love to Its Peak

Children, the one thing most people in this world pine for is love. A person searches for friends, gets married and leads a family life, all for love. However, tragically, love is the very thing most lacking in today's world. This is because everyone desires to receive love, but no one wants to give it. And even when love is given, it comes with a lot of expectations and conditions. Such "loving" relationships can shatter at any moment. The love can turn into hatred and hostility. This is the nature of the world. Once we understand this truth, we will not have to face sorrow. Heat and light are the nature of fire. We cannot think of fire with just one of these two attributes. Similarly, once we accept that there will be some sorrow in worldly love, then we will be able to accept anything and everything with equanimity.

There is pure love within all of us. There is also the ability to love everyone without expectations. Since love is our true nature, it is never lost. A gem lying immersed in oil appears to have lost its lustre. But the lustre can be restored. We just have to clean it. Similarly, we can restore ourselves to the purest form of love by removing our mental impurities.

Love is a ladder with many rungs. Today, most of us are standing on the lowest rung. We should not stay there for the rest of our life. Instead, use each rung as a steppingstone to reach the next. We should not stop until we reach the highest realm of love. This love is the ultimate goal of life.

"I love you" is a common expression. But it is incorrect. The truth is: "I am love. I am the embodiment of love." When we say, "I love you," there is an "I" and a "you." There is separation. Trapped in between this "you" and "I" is love. There it suffocates and eventually disappears.

Trying to love with the attitude of "I" and "you" is like a small snake trying to swallow a very big frog. Both suffer. But when love is expressed without any expectations, there is no suffering. Our selfless love helps awaken the selfless love in others as well. Then our lives become filled with love and happiness. Once we realise "I am the embodiment of love," we can never have any selfish desires or expectations. Just like a river flowing without any interruptions, our lives transform into pure love, flowing towards everyone. Then the world will reap only good things from us. May all of us rise to that highest realm of pure love.

Love Makes Our Life Divine

Children, many of us establish our relationship with others on the basis of profit and loss. In the midst of acquiring wealth, we often forget the wealth of love. Love is the wealth that makes our lives divine. Love is the real goodness of life.

In God's creation, many things are blessed with the ability to allure and make others happy. For example, the beauty of butterflies, the fragrance of flowers and the sweetness of honey attract everyone and spread happiness. This beauty, fragrance and sweetness come from within, not from outside. But what is the state of the most divine creation called human? If he needs fragrance on his body, he has to apply perfume. If he wants to be beautiful, he needs to put on good clothes and make-up. In spite of all of this, what comes from within humans are foul-smelling impurities. But if we try, we can spread happiness, comfort and good energy to others. The way to achieve this is through good thoughts, loving words, a smiling nature and selfless actions.

This life can end at any time. This awareness helps us to have right vision. Then, even when death stands before us, we will face it with happiness.

Doctors may tell patients with fatal diseases like cancer, "You will only live for three to six months." In that moment of seeing death before them, they realise that no material gain or fame will come with them and that their only salvation is in God. With that realisation, a big change happens within. They develop a mind that loves everyone. They want to forgive those who caused them pain. They seek forgiveness from those they have hurt.

Some such people have told Amma, "Amma, for the few days I have left, I want to live loving everyone. I have not been able to truly love my wife and children. Now I want to give them a lot of love. I want to love those who hate me and those whom I hated. Not only that, I have hurt many people, and I want to ask for their forgiveness as well."

All of us have the ability to love and forgive others like this. We don't have to wait for death to be on our doorstep. If we start today, we will be able to awaken this attitude.

It is not wealth or fame but love, compassion and caring that will make our life divine. Today, the human race needs this one realisation.

The Nature of the Guru

For the Subtlest Science, a Teacher Is Needed

Whether it is art, science, history or cooking a good meal—even tying a shoelace—one cannot learn anything without a teacher. Spirituality is a science—the science dealing with the inner self. As such, it is subtler than any other science. If one needs a teacher for all material sciences—which are grosser—than what to say of spirituality, the most subtle science of them all?

In fact, one does not really choose the *guru*. The relationship happens spontaneously—even more spontaneously than falling in love. However, for there to be a *guru*, there first must be a disciple. Once the disciple is ready, the *guru* just appears.

A *sadguru*—a true master—is completely devoid of ego. As such, he can make no claims. The *sadguru* will be the epitome of pure love, compassion and self-sacrifice. The *sadguru* will be humbler than the humblest and simpler than the simplest. In fact, in a true *guru*-disciple relationship, due to the incredible humility of the *guru*, it will be difficult to tell the difference between the *guru* and the disciple. Having transcended all sense of a separate individuality and all likes and dislikes, the *sadguru* can make no claims. Such a *guru* only sees divinity—the self-luminous self, pure awareness—in everything.

One day Darkness approached God and said, "I've never done anything to hurt the Sun, but he goes on torturing me. Wherever I go, he soon comes, and I have to run away. I never rest. I don't want to complain, but enough is enough! How long is this going to go on?"

God immediately summoned the Sun. God asked him, "Why are you harrassing poor Darkness?"

The Sun said, "What are you talking about? I've never met anything called Darkness." Sure enough, God looked around and Darkness was no longer there. He had disappeared. The Sun said, "Whenever you can manage to bring

Darkness in front of me, I'm ready to apologise or do whatsoever you say. Perhaps, unconsciously, I may have hurt him. But at least let me see him—this person who is complaining against me."

They say the file of Darkness' case against the Sun is still lying there. To date, God has yet to be able to bring both sides together before him. Sometimes Darkness comes; sometimes the Sun comes; but never both at the same time. Until both are present together, the case cannot be tried.

How can Darkness come to face the Sun? Darkness has no existence; it is just absence of light. So, where light is present, its absence cannot exist.

For us, who have no frame of reference regarding spirituality, the *guru* provides the necessary instructions, indications and clarity so that we can understand and assimilate the spiritual principles in their simplest and purest form.

Spirituality and spiritual thinking are the exact opposite of worldly life and material thinking. So, when we come to spiritual life with our old ways of thinking, what happens? We fail. It takes us a while to understand. However, the *guru,* is patient. He will explain and demonstrate, explain and demonstrate, explain and demonstrate over and over again, until we finally get it once and for all. If you want to learn a foreign language, the best way is to live with a native speaker. The *guru* is the native speaker of spirituality, of self-realisation.

The *guru* leads you from the known world of differences to the unknown world of oneness. A *sadguru* is established in total oneness with the Supreme. Therefore he sees divinity everywhere. When looking at the disciple, he sees the divine beauty lying dormant within. It is much like how a sculptor sees the beautiful statue trapped inside a rock. Just as the sculptor chisels away at the sharp edges of the rock to release the beautiful statue, so too does the *guru* work on the weaknesses and limitations of the disciple to help him realise his True Self.

In real surrender, there is no thinking because you transcend the mind. What we call "surrender" at present is just contemplating upon whether or not to surrender. In other words, while a disciple is undergoing training under a *sadguru*, there is still mental conflict and inner struggle. Only when the final state of surrender comes, does this conflict end and realisation take place. Surrender is not a "doing"; it is a "happening." It is an attitude that informs every aspect of the disciple's life.

Generally, there is a lot of fear associated with the word "surrender." Hearing it, we fear that in surrender we will lose everything. However, in reality, true surrender only brings us more clarity, more love, more compassion, more success—more of everything good, beautiful and wise. Surrender is like the seed losing its shell to become a tree.

Mahatmas Come Down to Raise Us Up

Children, spirituality is self-knowledge—the recognition of one's true nature. If a king is unable to recognise that he is the king, then his kingship is useless. If a beggar is unaware that there is valuable treasure under his hut, he will continue to live as a beggar. Most people are in a similar state. As such, in their desire for wealth and pleasure, they hurt each other and themselves. They even destroy Nature. If we want to uplift such people, we have to come down to their level.

Once, an oddly clothed magician arrived in a village. The villagers started poking fun at him. When they exceeded the limit of teasing, the magician got angry. He took some ash, chanted a mantra and dropped it into the village well. His curse was that anyone who drank the well water would go insane. This is exactly what happened. Soon everyone in the village was insane.

The village chief, however, had his own private well. He was fine. The villagers were completely mad. They would blurt out whatever nonsense came to their mind and dance around and behave insanely. They gradually noticed that their chief was not behaving like them. They were surprised. They decided that he was the insane one and tried to tie him up. It was total chaos. Somehow the chief escaped. He thought, "All the villagers have gone mad. They will not leave me alone if I behave differently from them. If I have to live here and uplift them, there is only one thing I can do: I must behave just like them. To catch a thief, one may have to act like one." With this resolve, the village chief began to dance and act just as crazy as the villagers. They were happy to see that their chief had been cured of his madness.

Gradually the village chief encouraged the villagers to dig another well and drink water from it. Eventually everyone returned to normal.

Mahatmas are like this village chieftain. People may poke fun at them. They may even label them "insane." But the *mahatmas,* who view praise and insult the same, do not concern themselves about these things. They reach down to the level of the people and uplift them by giving an example of service and love without expectation.

Spirituality is not blind belief in God or religious observances or customs. It is about uniting hearts. Only when our religion becomes spirituality will the society be established on a solid foundation of *dharma*, universal values and service-mindedness.

The Guru Is the Ultimate Truth Embodied

Children, some people think that surrendering to a *guru* is akin to becoming a slave—a form of bondage. Currently, we are like a king who one night dreamt he was a beggar and then became depressed. The *guru* wakes us up from the sleep of ignorance that is the very cause of all our sorrow.

Even if we've forgotten a poem we learnt as a youngster, it all comes back upon hearing someone recite the first few lines. Similarly, our current state is one of forgetfulness—a spiritual forgetfulness—and the *guru's* teachings hold the power to awaken us.

There is a tree in every seed. But for that tree to emerge, the seed must first go under the soil and break open. Similarly, even though we are that Infinite Truth, unless the shell of the ego breaks open, we will never experience that reality. The *guru* is the one who nurtures this process.

If a sapling is to grow into a tree, it needs a conducive environment. It needs to be watered at the right time, fertilised at the right time. It needs to be protected from various pests. The *guru* does the same thing for his disciples on a spiritual level, nurturing them and protecting them from the various obstacles and pitfalls.

Just as a filter purifies water, the *guru* purifies the disciple's mind, removing the ego. Currently we fall slave to the ego at every turn. We fail to use our discrimination and are thus unable to move forward in life.

Once, when a thief was breaking into a house, the people living there woke up, and he had to flee. The people in the house shouted, "Thief! Thief!" and soon a large crowd of people were all running after the thief. The clever thief got an idea. He also started to shout "Thief! Thief!" and then managed to slip in with the crowd and elude capture. This is how it is with the ego. It is difficult for the disciple to catch it and destroy it on his own. Education under a *sadguru* is essential.

The *guru* tries to completely remove the ego from the disciple. Surrendering to a *guru's* instructions is not an act of slavery but the path to supreme freedom and everlasting happiness. The *guru's* only goal is to completely free his disciple from sorrow. When the *guru* scolds him, the disciple may feel a little sad, but the *guru* scolds with only one aim—to uproot and destroy all the disciple's negative tendencies and awaken him to his True Self. During this process, the disciple will most likely experience some emotional pain. This pain is similar to the pain experienced when a doctor squeezes a wound in order to drain it of all the pus and bacteria inside. In order to get it all out, the doctor may even have to slice the wound open. To an uneducated onlooker, the doctor may seem cruel. But if, out of "sympathy" for the patient, the doctor forgoes this process and simply applies external medicine, the wound will never heal. Just as the doctor's only aim is to remove impurities from the physical body, the *guru's* only aim is to remove the negativities of the mind.

In reality, the *guru* is not a mere individual. He is the *parama tattvam*—the supreme principle. He is the embodiment of truth, renunciation, love and *dharma*. In the presence of a *sadguru*, the disciple is able to imbibe all the *guru* represents and liberate himself. This is the greatness of the *guru's* presence.

Our Culture

Respecting Our Elders

Children, one of the most important aspects of Indian culture is respecting and obeying our parents, teachers and elders. It used to be our habit to prostrate before our parents, to stand up in respect when they entered a room, and to give priority to those who were our seniors. It is sad to see that we have not maintained these habits and that we have failed to cultivate them in the next generation.

Some people ask, "Isn't giving priority and obedience a sign of weakness or slave mentality?" Children, never think like this. It is not so. These are practical ways to establish harmony in our families and society. For a machine to work dependably, we have to maintain it properly with oil, etc. Then it will always be ready to use. Similarly, in order to avoid friction between individuals and for society to move forward without obstacles, we must maintain good habits such as obeying our elders and giving them priority.

People respect authority figures. In reality, in doing so, we protect the laws of the country. Likewise, when we obey and respect people who are senior to us in age and knowledge, we are really respecting their wealth of experience. When a student shows respect to his teacher, it shows his desire to learn. It helps him to listen to the teacher's words with concentration and to fully internalise his lessons. Also, seeing the student's humility and curiosity, the teacher's heart melts. He wholeheartedly tries to bestow his knowledge on his student. It is really the student who gains the most by having respect and obedience.

Once, a person searched everywhere for a smooth, spherical stone to use for *puja*. He even climbed up a mountain, but he could not find even one smooth, spherical stone. In his frustration, he kicked a stone and it tumbled down the mountain. When he climbed down and reached the bottom of the mountain, he suddenly found a very nice, smooth, spherical stone. In reality, this was the very stone that he had kicked from the mountaintop. It had become smooth from colliding with other stones on its way to the bottom. Similarly, only when we drop the attitude of "I" and "mine" and attain obedience and simplicity will the sharp edges of our ego disappear. Only then will we acquire a mature mind.

Obedience is never an obstruction for free thinking and growth. When there is a new invention in science, there is free thinking. But what served as the foundation for this free thought was the precedence of the earlier scientists' work. Like this, only if every generation internalises the contributions of the previous generation with humility and obedience, will there be real progress.

Restoring the Harmony of Nature

Children, there is a rhythm to everything in this universe. The wind, the rain, the waves in the ocean, our breath, our heartbeats—each of these have their own rhythm. For our mental and physical health, and to ensure longevity, it is imperative this rhythm be maintained. It is our thoughts and actions that set the rhythm and melody to life. If the rhythm of our thoughts is lost, it will soon reflect in our actions. Sooner or later, this will impact the rhythm of Nature. The main cause of natural disasters like tsunamis, landslides and earthquakes is Nature's harmony gone awry.

Once a king wore a disguise and went on a hunting expedition. During the hunt, he became separated from the rest of his group and lost his way in the forest. Tired and hungry, he finally reached a hut—the home of a tribal family. They did not recognise the king. They brought him some fruits and berries. Biting into a fruit, the king exclaimed, "Oh, how bitter this fruit is!"

"Yes, it is very unfortunate," the tribal family agreed. "Our king is extremely selfish, self-indulgent and lecherous. In his cruelty, he forces us to pay excessive taxes. Those who cannot pay are put to death. Due to his *adharmic* deeds, even naturally sweet fruits are turning bitter."

When the king returned to his palace later that night, he could not forget the incident in the forest. He thought about how much his people were suffering because of him and was filled with remorse. He resolved to devote the rest of his life to sincerely serving his people. Soon, taxes were slashed and many charitable works and humanitarian activities were initiated.

After a few years, one day, he disguised himself and visited the old hut in the forest. The tribal family once again brought him fruits. This time, every one of the fruits was sweet. He asked the family the reason for this change. "Our ruler is a changed man," they responded. "He rules the kingdom very well now. The people are all happy and content. Due to his good deeds, there is a great change in Nature as well. This is why the fruits are so sweet."

What is the message of this story? Man's actions impact Nature. If his actions are *adharmic*, the balance of Nature will be lost. If his actions are *dharmic*, that will reflect in Nature as well. Nature's harmony will be restored.

Today, many people excessively exploit Nature. Hence, Nature is losing its rhythm. Natural disasters are becoming more and more common. Even small families prefer to live in large houses. Two people need only two rooms in a house. At most, all they can use is two or three extra rooms. But many people construct 10- or 15-room homes. For this, they level hills, blast mountains and drill bore-wells. They do not think twice about exploiting Nature for their selfish needs.

If we are a little careful, we can stop this excessive exploitation of our natural resources. Millions of people in our country travel to work alone in their cars. If five such people carpool, only 200 vehicles will be needed in place of a thousand. See how much we stand to gain by this! Traffic can be reduced drastically. Accidents will be less. Pollution will decrease. We can save on fuel consumption as well as fuel expenses. Furthermore, less traffic means less time commuting.

Man's senseless actions today remind us of the foolish woodcutter who tried to cut the very branch upon which he was sitting. It is crucial that our attitude changes. Protecting Nature is not man's duty to Nature; on the contrary, it is man's duty to himself. Man's very survival depends on Nature. When man and Nature move together in harmony, life becomes peaceful. When rhythm and harmony go together, the resulting music is melodious and pleasant to the ear. Similarly, when man lives in harmony with Nature, his life will become as sweet as a beautiful melody.

Welcome All "Unexpected Guests"

Children, our culture teaches us to view *atithis* [unexpected guests] as being equal to God. But by the word "unexpected guest" not only are people meant, but also each and every unexpected circumstance. Therefore, we must be prepared to view any circumstance that comes to us in life as a venerable guest and receive it happily.

In a game of chess, if we keep moving the pieces forward, we will not win. During certain circumstances, one may have to tactfully retract certain pieces. Similarly, when we encounter failure, we need to imbibe lessons from that experience and then use our newly gained knowledge to move forward.

When failure comes, we must be careful to limit that failure to the external. We cannot allow our mental strength and self-confidence to fail as well. Secondly, we should never abandon our good-heartedness and service-mindedness.

Once, campus interviews were being conducted at a management institute. After the interviews were over, the students returned to their rooms. A few students emerged successful. They were very happy. The others were sad. One of the unselected students remained seated in the interview hall. There was a gentle breeze there. He sat there for some time, enjoying the breeze. The chairs there were now strewn helter-skelter about the room. He noticed that and decided to rearrange all of them into proper order.

As he was doing this, he noticed someone watching him from the doorway. It was one of the interviewers. The actions of this youth had caught his attention. Instead of feeling sad about failing, the boy remained focused and maintained a sense of social responsibility. Seeing the boy's work the interviewer felt respect for the boy. He called the young man to his side and gave him a well-paying job.

It was the young man's undefeated sense of social responsibility and his presence of mind that landed him the job. He was not worried too much about not getting the job. Instead, he thought about what he could do in that present moment. It wasn't his job to clean the hall. But he did not think, "This is not my job; let someone else do it." Even though it was not his job, he carried it out beautifully. This high-minded attitude took him to victory.

Not all who act like this youth will end up victorious. But it is the unbreakable law of the universe that those who do good deeds definitely reap their benefits—if not today, then tomorrow.

A Light in This Darkness

Children, the state of the world today is very sad. On one side, terrorism and terrorist attacks are without end. On the other side, because of man's selfishness and greed, natural disasters are happening with more and more frequency. Still, even in these circumstances, we can see rays of hope here and there. There are people who try very hard to help those who are hungry and suffering. These people are our role-models because their compassion-filled hearts awaken hope for a bright future.

Amma is reminded of an incident that happened years ago during a foreign tour. During *darshan*, a 13-year-old boy gave me a small envelope. Hugging him, Amma asked "What is it?"

The boy said, "300 euros."

"Where did you get this from, son?"

"I took part in a flute competition. I got first prize. This is the prize money. Amma takes care of many orphans, and this will help them in some way."

Listening to his words and seeing his innocent heart, Amma had tears in her eyes. Amma said, "Son, your goodness has filled Amma's heart today. People like you are Amma's real wealth."

But the story doesn't end there. The boy's younger sister became very sad. She also wanted to do something for the poor people, just like her brother. Two weeks later, those children came to see Amma again. When they came for *darshan*, the little sister gave Amma an envelope. Amma asked, "Daughter, what's in this envelope?"

Her mother answered. "It was her birthday a week ago. When her grandfather gave her 10 euros, she had one strong desire: She wanted to give the money to Amma to buy chocolates for the orphans." Listening to this, Amma hugged this beautiful child, kissing her.

Amma asked her, "Doesn't my daughter want to eat ice cream and chocolate?"

The girl shook her head, "No."

"Why not?" Amma asked.

The girl said, "I get to eat that all the time. But aren't there a lot of children who don't have money to buy these things? Amma must take this money and buy them chocolates."

Her brother, in his compassion-filled action, had become a role-model for this young girl. May these compassion-filled little hearts become role-models for all of us.

Change has to start from within individuals. As change happens in individuals, there will be changes in families too. Society will then progress. So, first, we must try to change ourselves. We must make certain that through all of our actions, we become role-models for others.

Spiritual Practices & Vedic Science

Samadhi

Children, the easiest and most scientific method to help our mind achieve one-pointed focus is meditation. When meditation becomes completely one-pointed, it is known as *samadhi*.

The mind is a constant flow of thoughts. *Samadhi* is the state wherein all thoughts disappear, all desires are contained, and the mind becomes totally still. In *samadhi*, the mind merges into the pure consciousness that is its foundation—into pure awareness alone. That experience is supreme peace, supreme bliss.

Once Goddess Parvati told Lord Siva, "I feel lonely when you are wandering around the world, begging for alms. Since you abide in the constant state of *samadhi*, you may not feel any sadness due to our separation. But I am not like that. I cannot bear this separation from you. So,

I beg you to teach me what *samadhi* is. Then, I won't have to suffer from missing you so much."

Lord Siva asked Parvati Devi to sit in a lotus posture, close her eyes and turn her mind inward. Devi became absorbed in meditation. Lord Siva then asked, "What do you see now?"

Devi replied, "I see your form in my mind's eye."

"Go beyond that form. Now what do you see?"

"A divine effulgence."

"Go beyond even that. Now?"

"I perceive only sound now."

"Go beyond that. What is your experience now?"

There was no answer. Devi's individuality itself had been totally absorbed. It had disappeared. Devi had completely merged with Lord Siva. There was no individual there anymore to answer. Devi had reached everlasting, indivisible union with her Lord. She was in the realm of pure love, where the mind, words, ideas and thoughts cannot enter.

There are several types of *samadhi*. One may experience the merging of the mind for a short period of time during deep meditation. During these meditations, one will experience peace and bliss. But this state is not permanent. When the meditation ends, the thoughts will rise again. On the other hand, a truly enlightened master will experience constant *samadhi*—even while transacting in the world. This is called *sahaja samadhi*.

In *sahaja samadhi*, there is only bliss. There is no sorrow or happiness. There is no "I" or "you." This is when the mind is in an everlasting Self-realised state. *Sahaja samadhi* is beyond time and space. It continues under all circumstances, no matter what one is doing. Even while sleeping there is no change in this state. One will always exist as pure consciousness. In others' view, they will continue to be of this world, in duality. However, in truth, they will be constantly revelling in their own pure awareness, pure consciousness—the Self. Such individuals are the very embodiment of supreme consciousness.

In their presence, others will also experience bliss, joy and consolation.

Yoga Versus Physical Exercise

Children, *yoga* is a way to awaken the infinite power within us through proper integration of mind, body and intellect and to ultimately realise our own full potential. *Yoga* is also helpful in increasing our patience, health, mental happiness and awareness of values. Due to the increase in lifestyle-induced diseases and mental-health issues, we find the popularity of *yoga* spreading throughout the world. Every Indian citizen can take pride in knowing that *yoga* is a science that was born and developed in our country.

Many people want to know the special benefits of *yoga* compared to other forms of exercise. Any type of exercise is helpful in restoring physical and mental health, but the benefits derived from *yoga* are far superior to those of ordinary exercise. Ordinary exercises lower the fat levels of the body and enhance muscular strength through fast physical movements. But *yoga* concentrates more on giving rest to all parts of the body and in proper redirecting the life-force energy. This paves the way to proper functioning of all the internal organs and glands and curing diseases. The nerves become purified. It increases mental strength and helps us to gain one-pointed concentration. Muscles become flexible and strong. Compared to the other exercises, *yoga* decreases depression and establishes a happy mental state.

Yoga positions are also different from other exercises. They are done deliberately, carefully concentrating on the breath, observing each movement of the body. Through this, the mind becomes peaceful and can approach at an experience like meditation. Thus, *yoga* helps the body and mind equally.

To cure a person suffering from a chronic illness, apart from medicines, he also needs proper food and rest. Similarly, for *yoga* to be whole and perfect, it should be part of a disciplined and value-based lifestyle. Through performing *yoga* with total awareness, it gradually becomes possible to do every action with awareness. This leads to improved thoughts and emotions. Gradually, by acquiring one-pointedness in meditation and other actions, we will be able to realise our True Self.

Yoga supports seeing unity in diversity and nonviolence towards all living things. Thus, the popularity of *yoga* can help love and friendship grow in society and foster world peace.

Astrology & Faith in God

Children, many people become addicted to astrology due to their anxiety and fear over the future. There is no dearth of people who panic and worry about subjects like marriage, business, their job, promotions and so on. The favourable and unfavourable situations we face in this life are primarily caused by actions we have performed in past lives. While astrology can give us hints about our fate and recommend various means to mitigate our negative experiences, it cannot prevent them entirely. Therefore, it is important that we make our mind capable of enduring problems with equanimity.

Once a *mahatma* gave two idols to a king and said, "Be very careful with these idols. If they break, big calamities will befall the kingdom. There may be war or famine or floods." The king entrusted the idols with a servant who kept them very carefully in a special place.

One day, one of the idols happened to break. The servant immediately informed the king, who became irate and imprisoned him.

A few days later, a neighbouring king attacked the kingdom with a huge army. The king blamed the servant and ordered him to be hung. When asked whether he had any last wish, the servant said, "Before I die, I should be allowed to break the second idol."

Hearing this, the king asked him, "Why are you saying this?"

The servant said, "It is because the first idol broke that you are having me executed. Another innocent person should not be forced to die because of the other idol. The *mahatma* who gave those idols to you said that if the idols break, bad things will happen. He did not say that bad things will happen because the idols broke. The breaking of the idol merely indicated that a war was about to start. As soon as you received that hint, you should have immediately prepared to face the enemy king's army."

Hearing this, the king realised his mistake and freed the servant.

Astrology and omens merely indicate the hardships or good fortune that could occur in our life. There is no point in blaming the planets or God for our difficulties and problems. We should remain alert and ensure that all our present actions are good. If we do this, then our future will also be full of goodness.

Even atheists and sceptics have immense faith in astrologers and soothsayers! A good, intuitive astrologer may be able to recount your past and make fairly accurate predictions about your future. More than an astrologer's scholarship is his ability to tune his mind with the higher realms. Ultimately it is the divine grace he is taps into that gives accuracy to his predictions.

Similarly, ultimately only God's grace can change a situation or an experience we are karmicly fated to undergo. It is also important to remember that no karmic situation can be averted completely. Regardless, our prayers, meditation and spiritual practices certainly have a positive impact.

Many people think hiring priests to do *pujas* and *homas* will help. While such rituals are very powerful, the sincere and dedicated effort we put into our own spiritual and religious observances is more important.

Astrology is part of the Vedic culture. It is a science—a pure and subtle mathematical calculation based on the relationship between the movements of the solar system, nature and the human mind. Like all other ancient scriptures, astrological knowledge also dawned in the hearts of the *rishis* during their deep meditations—a state when their mind was one with the universe and its unsullied and unconditioned vibrations. Thus, let us understand that our faith should neither be in the astrologer nor in his predictions, but in that ultimate governing power of this universe, God. The unintelligent and undiscerning actions we've performed in the past should be counterbalanced with intelligent and discerning actions in the present. If we do so, the future will become our friend.

Much more helpful than trying to change situations is trying to change our perception. Adverse circumstances and hardships are often unavoidable. We should try our best to be on the right path, to act and think in a *dharmic* manner. If negative experiences still come our way after our sincere attempts to circumvent

141

them, then we should have the attitude to accept them as the will of God. Only then will there be peace and tranquillity in life.

Values

Avoid Preconceptions

Children, we perceive some people as "good," and we brand others "worthless." Then, after a while, we change our mind. Those we called "good" before we now call "bad" and vice-versa. Thus, our opinions and perspectives are in a constant state of flux. Why? The main reason is that we lack proper knowledge. It is our habit to judge everything through preconceived notions.

When we view something through the lens of our preconceived notions, we will fail to correctly understand it. We should view everything in its proper place and should learn to look at things with an open mind. Only then can we understand the reality of a situation.

This world and the objects and individuals in it are undergoing constant change. The individual we saw yesterday is different from the individual we see today. A tailor always takes fresh measurements, even for regular customers. He never thinks, "Oh, I took this person's measurement the last time he was here. There's no need to do it again." He knows that the dimensions of the customer's body, as well as his likes and dislikes, are subject to change. We should have a similar attitude when we interact with others. A person's behaviour and his attitude towards us may change at any moment. Today's foe could easily become tomorrow's friend. Today's friend could also become tomorrow's foe. We should always see others with an open mind, without preconceived notions.

Some people think acting based on preconceived notions can prevent future difficulties. However, in reality, that requires not preconceptions, but attention. Preconception is negative; attention is positive. When we act with preconceptions, we lose the opportunity to learn new things. But working with attention reveals many new ideas and perspectives will be.

Once, a man's wallet with a large amount of money went missing. He had last seen it just a short while before in its proper place in his room. The man, his wife and children searched the house from top to bottom but could not find it. At this time, the seven-year-old son suddenly piped up, "The boy next door was here a little while ago." Suddenly the entire family became suspicious of the neighbour's boy, whom they had previously only viewed with love. "Haven't you noticed his sly look?" they told each other. "There is no doubt he did it." They began to feel that he looked, walked and acted like a thief. Their love and trust in him quickly evaporated. They also began to view the other members of the boy's family with contempt. Gradually, they lost their peace of mind.

A week or so later, the wife was giving the house a thorough cleaning. Suddenly, she discovered the lost wallet under a sofa cushion. Her attitude towards the neighbour's boy changed instantly. He once again became the sweet, innocent boy of the past. When we view anything with preconceptions, our mind makes a premature judgement. Thereafter, everything is cast in the light of that judgment. Often, we are wrong. Therefore, before we form a conclusion, we should first observe the situation with attention and discrimination. This is the correct path.

In fact, preconceptions often form when we project our own likes and dislikes upon others. This doesn't help us to see the truth but, rather, blinds us. Preconceptions force us to view the world through their tinted lens. Depending on the colour of the filter, we begin to think of the world as "blue," "black" or "green," etc. Thus, real insight into the nature of the world becomes impossible. We should understand and evaluate the world, our circumstances, our experiences and ourselves with attention and maturity, not with preconceived notions. Only through spirituality can this be achieved.

Awaken Awareness

Children, today we have knowledge but no awareness. We have intellect but no discrimination. Our thoughts, words and actions should arise from right knowledge and clear awareness. Otherwise, we will not reach our intended goals. If a cart is pulled by horses going in opposite directions, it will not reach anywhere. However, if both horses pull the cart in the same direction, it will reach the destination very quickly. Similarly, we will only progress quickly in life if our thoughts, words and actions are in alignment.

As long as our awareness is not awakened, we will not be able to properly make use of even the fortunate circumstances that come our way in life. We will act without thinking and end up in disaster.

Once a businessman bought a factory that was on the brink of bankruptcy and closure. For the factory to succeed, he needed to get rid of any lazy and thieving workers and replace them with able, sincere and truthful workers.

He started observing all the factory workers with keen eyes. On his first visit, he saw a worker leaning against a wall, sleeping. Next to him were a group of workers doing their work. Deciding to teach everyone a lesson, the businessman woke the sleeping man and asked, "What's your monthly salary?"

The man opened his eyes and, with a surprised look, said, "6,000 rupees."

Immediately, the factory owner opened his purse, took out a handful of money and gave it to the man, saying, "Ordinarily, when a worker is dismissed from his job, he is given two months' salary. But I am giving you four months'. Here is 24,000 rupees. I don't want to see you anywhere around here from now on."

After the man left, the businessman asked the other workers, "Which department did he work in?"

One of them responded, "He doesn't work here, sir. He brought lunch for someone and was waiting to collect the containers."

In this story, the owner was very intelligent, but his actions lacked awareness. Because of this, he became the object of ridicule.

For any action to be done with complete awareness, five factors must come together. First is knowledge about one's own work. Two, the power to discern between right and wrong and to see all the possible outcomes. Three, a calm and peaceful mind. Four, complete focus. And five, the detachment to remove oneself, stand back and view ourselves and our actions objectively. When these five factors come together, we will be able to do any work to the best of our ability. May our efforts be for that.

Bad Habits

Children, one of the most dangerous things that can happen to us is to fall into the clutches of bad habits. Once that happens, it is very difficult to get free. So, we must always remain vigilant.

It is when we repeatedly engage in negative thinking and actions that they become habits. Without our knowledge, these habits then devour our very life.

Once, a man went to the eye doctor because of irritation in his eyes. After examining him, the doctor said, "There's nothing to worry about. Just flush your eyes with brandy twice a day. Within one week, the discomfort will go away." Next week, the patient returned to the doctor. After examining him, the doctor said, "There's no improvement! What happened? Didn't you follow my instructions?" The patient said, "I tried but it was impossible to get my hand past my mouth."

When habits become our nature, we fall slave to those habits. The influence of habits on us is that powerful.

Today we are in a kind of sleep state. Because of this, we have no awareness with regards to our words and actions. It's not enough to have knowledge; our awareness must be awakened. Only then will we get the full benefit from our knowledge. Everyone who smokes knows that smoking is injurious to their health, but they still smoke. Only when they get diagnosed with cancer will the awareness of just how bad the habit is awaken in them. Then, even if they desire to smoke, they will not touch a cigarette again.

Many people with bad habits tell me, "This habit has formed over years. It's very hard to stop it just like that. So, I will try to stop it little by little." This is because they fail to realise just how dangerous their bad habit is to their physical and mental health. Imagine a house that has caught fire while the owner is sleeping. He wakes up to see fire completely surrounding him. His only thought will be to escape. He will not take his sweet time. Similarly, the moment we really understand that bad habits injure us, we will drop them instantly.

The first thing we need to free ourselves from our bad habits is determination. The second is to avoid tempting situations. It is important to stay away from friends that lead us to wrongdoing. Don't hesitate to get help from a physician or a counsellor when it is needed. If you have vigilance and make constant effort, you can overcome any bad habit.

Devotion Is an End in Itself

Children, the common belief is that God incarnates in human form to protect and preserve *dharma* and annihilate *adharma*. But even beyond that, there is another reason God incarnates. That is to awaken love for Him in human hearts. This is why many sages say that in addition to the four goals of human life—righteousness, financial security, desire and liberation—there is a fifth goal: devotion.

A true devotee does not even desire liberation. He has only one goal: "May I always remember and serve God." He doesn't desire anything else. According to the real devotee, devotion is an end in itself. In the devotion to pursue devotion, the individual ceases to exist. With this, surrender becomes complete. Even then, the desire to enjoy loving God remains in the devotee's heart. By enjoying the bliss of devotion constantly, the devotee also becomes an embodiment of bliss.

Once, Uddhava said to the Lord, "I've heard that among all devotees, you love the *gopikas* the most. There are many other devotees who become tear-eyed the moment they hear your name. They go into *samadhi* when they hear your divine flute. When they see the blue hue of your divine body—even way in the distance—they are overcome and swoon. What then is so great about the devotion of the *gopikas*?"

Upon hearing this, the Lord smiled and said, "All my devotees are dear to me. But the *gopikas* have something very special and unique. Other devotees shed tears when they hear my name. But the *gopikas* hear all names as my name. For them, all sounds are Lord Krishna's divine flute. Any colour appears as blue in their eyes. The *gopikas* are able to see oneness in diversity. This is why they have become the dearest to me."

A wife who loves her husband as her own life thinks about her dear husband as she picks up the pen to write to him. Her mind is filled with his memories alone as she fills the pen with ink and picks the paper upon which to write. Similarly, a true devotee's mind is constantly on God—as he gets ready for worship, as he prepares the vessels, incense sticks, camphor and flowers. In that supreme, noble moment of devotion, he sees the Creator in all of creation. For this reason alone, the *gopikas* were unable to see anything as different from their Lord.

May the memories of Lord Krishna and the *gopikas*—dancing blissfully in Vrindavan, forgetting everything else in their delight—fill our hearts with devotion, delight and bliss.

Action & Thought

Children, there two types of people in this world—ones who act without thinking and ones who think without acting. The first group gets into a lot of trouble by acting without thinking—or at least without thinking correctly. Not only do they fail to help anyone, but they also often harm people. The second group thinks with discrimination and understands what is right and what is wrong. However, they do not act accordingly. At most, they may advise others. This is like a sick person asking someone else to take medicine on his behalf. We often plan to undertake many virtuous acts, but then we create many excuses to cancel our plan.

Once there was an ancient temple. Every week, a large group of devotees would go there for meditation and prayers. Watching this, a monkey thought to himself, "All these devotees receive God's grace by doing austerities and prayers. Why can't I also do some fasting and meditation too?" The next prayer day, this monkey sat under a tree and started to meditate.

Immediately he thought: "I have never done fasting like this before. By the time the day of fasting ends, I may be too tired to even walk. I could die! If I sit under a fruit tree, then I won't have to go far looking for food after I'm done."

Thinking like this, the monkey got up and sat under a fruit tree. Then he started to meditate. After a while, he started thinking, "After fasting for so long, what if I don't have any energy to climb the tree to get the fruit?" So, he climbed up to a branch that had a lot of fruit on it and sat there to meditate. Then he thought, "What if my arms are too weak to pluck the fruits after fasting?" So, he plucked a lot of fruit, held it in his lap and started to meditate again. A little while later, he felt hungry. He thought, "I haven't had such big and tasty fruit in a long time. I can always fast another day!" As soon as this thought entered his mind, the fruit was in his mouth.

Many of us are like this monkey. Our mind will constantly find excuses to avoid doing what needs to be done. Along with knowledge, we must have determination and one-pointed focus on our goal. Those who have mental will power and work towards fulfilling all their goals will definitely succeed.

Don't Fall Slave to Anger

Children, anger is a weakness that makes us a slave. When we become angry, we lose both our self-control and proper judgment. We lose all awareness of ourselves and of what we are saying and doing.

Today, our mind has become like a puppet in the hands of others. They know exactly how to push our buttons. If they praise us, we become happy. If they criticise us, we become agitated. Thus, our life is controlled by the words of others. Furthermore, when we start jumping up and down in anger, creating a hell for those close to us, it becomes a real source of entertainment for onlookers!

This reminds me of a story: A man went to a barbershop. Soon after the barber began cutting his hair, he said to the man, "You know, I met your mother-in-law yesterday. Do you know what she said? She said that you've stashed away quite a bit of black money."

Hearing this, the man's face turned red with anger. "Did she say that? She is no better than a common thief! Do you know how many people she has borrowed money from without ever paying back a single paisa? I'm the one who repays all her debts!" The man did not stop there. He continued to badmouth his mother-in-law throughout the entire haircut.

A month or so later, when the man went to have his hair cut again, the barber seated him in the chair, picked up his scissors and immediately started in about his mother-in-law. "I ran into your mother-in-law the other day," he said. "She told me that you don't give her any money for household expenses."

The man became enraged. He started shouting, "Who is that demoness to say such a thing! It is I who bear all her expenses—her clothes, her food, everything!" Once set off like this, he, again, continued his diatribe against his mother-in-law throughout the duration of his haircut.

The third time he went for a haircut, the barber again brought up his mother-in-law. This time, the man stopped him and said, "Hey, why do you always mention my mother-in-law? I don't want to hear about her anymore."

The barber responded. "Well, you see, I mention her because it makes you so angry that your hair stands on end. Then, it's very easy to cut your hair."

When we become angry, the anger becomes our master, and we become its slave. But with proper understanding and self-control, we can change this. When we understand that our anger is a weakness, we can begin to make efforts to control it.

In reality, every person and every circumstance are mirrors, reflecting our weaknesses and negativities. Just as we wash the dirt off our face while looking into a mirror, so too we should use all the various circumstances that come to us in life to wash away the dirt of all of our weaknesses and negativities.

If we gain spiritual understanding, it will become much easier for us to have self-control over our emotions and thoughts. If anyone becomes angry with us, we should remember that anger is a handicap—a mental handicap.

This will help us to forgive the person. Or we can contemplate, "What is the point in becoming angry in return? Wouldn't it be wiser if, instead, I put in effort to conquer this ego of mine, which is the real source of all the pain I am feeling?" If we can reflect in this manner, we will be able to maintain our mental equanimity and remain composed at all times.

Enthusiasm Is the Secret to Success

Children, no matter what field we want to succeed in, we need tireless enthusiasm. No matter what obstacles we face, we have to persevere. We have to keep trying with constant enthusiasm and self-confidence. Someone who is always enthusiastic will always succeed.

A toddler falls so many times, but he always quickly gets up and tries to walk again. No matter how many times he stumbles and falls, he always gets up. Even if gets bruised or hurt, he will continue to try. And it is as a result of his unflagging effort, enthusiasm and patience that he learns to walk. When facing obstacles, we should persist like this child without feeling crushed.

Once, a herd of goats saw there was a vast vineyard on a mountaintop. All the goat kids became incredibly excited. They could think of nothing but dashing up the mountain to eat the grapes! They all started climbing as fast as they could. Seeing this, the older goats said, "Hey, where are you going? That vineyard is up so high! You'll never be able to get up there." Hearing these words, the kids began losing their enthusiasm. Soon they became tired and, one by one, started climbing back down. In the end, only one goat kid remained. It just kept climbing. All the goats and goat kids below tried their best to get that lone goat kid to come back, but none of them could dampen his enthusiasm. Eventually, he reached the mountaintop and ate grapes to his heart's content. When he came back down, all his friends clapped and received him with much fanfare. Watching all this, one goat asked, "Amazing! How were you able to do it when no one else could?" The goat kid didn't respond. Then his mother said, "My kid is deaf."

In fact, the goat kid's deafness turned into a blessing. He was able to remain enthusiastic despite being surrounded by criticism.

We all have this same power to prevail within us. Unfortunately, most of us collapse in the face of negativity and never recognise this wondrous inner strength. We should be alert and make sure that we always retain focus upon our life's goal. If there is awareness of our goal and constant effort, we will be able to achieve seemingly impossible feats.

Healing From Guilt Over Past Mistakes

Children, a lot of people in this world walk around feeling guilty about all the mistakes they've made, knowingly and unknowingly. Many of them succumb to depression and other mental problems. Some of them even commit suicide. Many people who visit temples and go on pilgrimages are looking for forgiveness from their wrongdoings. But very few find true peace from the guilt that haunts their mind.

Wallowing in regret and sadness over mistakes we've made can be compared to hugging and crying over a dead body. No matter how much we cry, it will not return to life. Similarly, no matter how much we try, we can never go back in time and undo our mistakes. Time only moves forward.

When children get a small cut, they usually scratch it repeatedly and make the wound worse. Eventually they can no longer stand the pain. Repeatedly telling yourself, "I made these mistakes.

I am a sinner" is just like this. It transforms a small wound into serious disease. It will never bring peace of mind.

In any circumstance, we must think practically. If we happen to fall, we must not stay on the ground, crying. Simply get up and continue to walk. Take every step with caution. Don't lose hope.

A reporter asked a famous farmer, "What is the secret of your success?"

The farmer answered, "Taking right decisions."

Again the reporter asked, "How were you able to make right decisions?"

"Experience."

"How did you gain experience?"

"From making wrong decisions."

The practical experience the farmer received from making wrong decisions helped him make the right decisions. Then, when he made the right decisions, he succeeded. This farmer's story teaches us that even wrong decisions become steppingstones to success.

This present moment is the only wealth we possess. Only in the present moment can we undo our mistakes and follow the path of goodness. When we become sad thinking about the past, we are wasting the invaluable present moment.

What is most important is how well we use the present. This is what dictates our life's path. Therefore, take a solid oath not to repeat your mistakes. If it is possible, take the necessary steps to undo past mistakes or make amends. Then walk ahead with focus on your goal. This is what is needed.

In Our Rush, Beauty Is Lost

Children, we are living at a time when we cannot put aside time for others or ourselves. The reason is that our mind is constantly occupied by hundreds of thoughts—thoughts about things that happened in the past, about things that may happen in the future, about things we have to get done. Because of this, we are unable to understand what needs to be done in the present; we are unable to act in a way that brings good results. As a result, we have no peace; we miss the beauty of this world.

A grandfather and his grandson would regularly go for walks in a nearby flower garden. One day, while walking, the grandson felt something hard under the dry leaves. He bent down to see what it was and found a coin. "Someone must have dropped this while walking here," he said and joyfully picked it up. From then on, whenever they took their walk, the boy would scan the dry leaves for coins. Every now and then, he would find one or two and put them in his pocket. He did not inform his grandfather about this.

When they got home, he would put the coins safely in a container. This became a habit. About five years later, the boy showed the container to his grandfather saying, "Grandpa, look at all the coins I collected during our walks! It's more than 100 rupees!"

The boy's grandfather smiled and said, "Son, you are lucky to have found so many coins. But think of all the things you missed while you were busy looking for coins. You never saw the beautiful trees swaying in the wind. You never heard the birds singing their melodious songs. So many sunrises and sunsets have gone by without you noticing. So many flowers blossoming, so many rainbows! You missed the sound of the running brooks, the beauty of the ponds. Son, such things are priceless."

Isn't this too often how it is in our lives? Many people bring their family to the beach to see the sunset. Regardless, they keep checking their email and text messages. In the midst of all that beauty, they never enjoy it. We spend so much time on Facebook, yet fail to see the faces of the people next to us.

Children, it shouldn't be like this. Technology is fine. It can bring us closer to those who are far away, but it shouldn't take us away from those who are close. Often the wife is obviously so sad, but the husband never even notices. Working day and night, fathers shouldn't fail to take time to listen to the stories of the family. What a pity it is if we have a beautiful garden, but every time we sit in it, we just talk on the phone and never enjoy its beauty.

Mental agitation can easily eclipse the beauty of this world. Then, life becomes like a beautiful flower covered in mud. Only if thoughts come in the right manner, at the right time, can we accomplish our tasks peacefully and live in the present. Only then, can we enjoy the beauty that is both our true nature and the nature of the world.

Learn to Give Back to Society

Children, until recently, self-sacrifice and simplicity were considered two of the most important aspects of life. However, today the primary aim of most people is simply to make as much money as possible and to accumulate as many material possessions as possible. Tragically, people think success is taking the maximum and giving the minimum.

When we take something from nature or from society, it is our responsibility to give something back. If we make sure that we give more than we take, then there will be permanent peace, prosperity and unity in society. But, today, people maintain a business relationship with society and nature. They even have a business relationship with God. We are supposed to try to cultivate an attitude of surrender towards God, but instead, even when people pray, they try to make a profit.

Once a rich businessman was sailing on a ship. Suddenly the ship encountered a terrible storm. The captain announced that the chances of survival were slim. Everyone started to pray. The businessman started praying, "God, if I survive, I will sell my five-star hotel and give 70 per cent of the money to you. Please protect me!" Amazingly, as soon as he said this, the sea calmed down. Soon, all of the passengers, including the businessman, were safely on shore. But now the businessman was in agony. He started thinking, "If I sell my hotel, I will get at least 10 million rupees, and I will have to give seven million to God. How horrible!" He started trying to think of a way out. The next day, an advertisement appeared in all the newspapers. It said: "Five Star Hotel for Sale for Only One Rupee." Hundreds of people came out to try to buy the hotel. The businessman stood up and said, "Okay. It's true that I'm selling the hotel for one rupee. But there is one condition. The person who buys the hotel must also buy my puppy. And the price of the puppy is ten million rupees." Eventually a buyer came forward, the sale was completed and the businessman offered 70 paisa to God.

This is the attitude of many people in today's world. To get what we want, we are even ready to cheat God.

Today, we look at everything through the eyes of a businessman. Our only concern is our own selfish interests—whatever be the field. Because of this, many people think they are growing. But such growth is like a form of cancer—an unbalanced growth that ultimately leads to both the destruction of the individual and the society. Individual growth that fails to considerate the growth of society cannot be called true growth. Our growth should not prevent others from growing. On the contrary, it should help others to grow.

Children, whatever we give to the world will come back to us. If we sow one seed, the earth will return it to us a hundred-fold. Whatever we give will come back to us as blessing both in the present and in the future. Our lives become richer not by taking, but by giving.

Overcoming Tension

Children, today, people are in constant tension. Even with all life's comforts, people cannot escape from tension. Constant worry has become our nature.

Merely looking at a cut on our hand, worrying and crying about it, will not heal it. We should wash and clean the wound and apply medicine. Otherwise, it may get infected. It is the same with problems. Just worrying about them will not solve them.

In fact, worrying over our problems just magnifies them. It then becomes like running a race with a hundred-kilo weight around our neck. How can we win? Our life will be miserable.

Normally, a healthy person's blood pressure will have a low of 80 and high of 120. When a person with high blood pressure gets stressed, it will increase to 150 or 200. Such a person can have a stroke and become paralysed on one side. Tension weakens us, inside and out. A good percentage of people in society have heart disease. Many wear a pacemaker. If we can install the "peacemaker" of spirituality, however, most pacemakers will not be needed.

Once, a *guru* and his disciples were walking in the sun. When they saw a tree, they sat in its shade. The *guru* asked the disciples to bring some water. In the distance, they saw a small pond. But when they began to collect water there in a pot, a farmer brought his bulls to bathe. The water became completely muddy. The disciples were disheartened and returned to the *guru* and told him what had happened. The *guru* asked them to sit next to him. Everyone rested for a half hour in the shade. After that, the *guru* said, "Now, go back to the pond and check." The disciples went back to the pond and saw that the water was now crystal clear. They filled their pots and offered it to the *guru*. The *guru* said, "This is the condition of the human mind. When problems arise, it gets murky and agitated. But by being quiet and silent for some time, it becomes calm again. Then it regains all its talents and capabilities."

Simple Living and Self-Sacrifice

Children, our society's outlook and values are radically changing. Until two generations ago, simple living and self-sacrifice were our highest ideals. However, today most consider luxury the most important thing. Wastefulness and extravagance have become part of our lifestyle.

Some people spend thousands—tens of thousands—of rupees on extra comfort and extravagance. At the same time, their neighbours are starving. A thousand rupees can be the difference between a girl getting married or living a life alone. Some spend hundreds of thousands of rupees to celebrate their daughter's wedding. Other families reject their daughter-in-law, sending her back to her parents because she did not bring enough dowry. There are so many incidents of such things.

These days, Indians tend to be very extravagant when it comes to weddings. In truth, weddings can be conducted simply, in front of a registrar. Even so, a wedding represents unity and auspiciousness. In olden days, wedding celebrations were to make neighbours and friends happy so that they would lavish blessings upon the newlyweds and, thereby, fill the new couple's life with the nectar of peace and happiness. All that has changed over time.

We should not give such importance to external extravagance. With a little compassion in our hearts, we can reduce the amount of money we spend on our own child's wedding and give what we save to help poor girls get married.

Today, Indian society—especially Kerala society—is obsessed with gold. Our society has taught us that the Malayalam word *penn* not only means "woman" but also means "gold." These days some women go around wearing more gold than an elephant wearing *nettipattam* [the golden headdress put on elephants during festival ceremonies]. Women generally believe they are incomplete without gold draped around their wrists and neck. It has become an external expression of one's pride.

Amma would never say that purchasing gold is wrong. When gold is bought after thinking carefully, it can become a good investment. But being obsessed with gold is dangerous—especially when parents borrow money or sell or pawn property to cover wedding expenses. Actually, this obsession with gold is not created by women, but by society.

We must maintain balance and simplicity in all our actions. Everything has its place. At the same time, exceeding certain limits, anything can become *adharma*. Exploiting the earth's natural resources without regard for others is a sin. When bathing or washing dishes, we should be careful not to use more water than we really need. We should turn off lights and ceiling fans when we leave a room. We should never waste food. We must be careful with these things. So many people throughout the world are starving.

Our lives will become blessed if we shift our focus from fulfilling our own desires to helping others. If we are ready to end our bad habits and cut down on extravagance, we can use the money we save to help the suffering—people who cannot even afford one decent meal a day. Then, the light of goodness will not only illumine their lives, but also our own.

Sympathy Versus Compassion

Children, at first glance, sympathy and compassion seem to be only slightly different. However, when we really examine them, we see that they are very different. Sympathy is a momentary feeling we get when we see someone in despair. It doesn't have much impact on the suffering person. The sympathising person offers the suffering person some help, perhaps says a few comforting words, and this makes him feel good about himself. Compassion, on the other hand, is experiencing someone else's sorrow as our own. There is no duality in compassion—only oneness. When the left hand gets hurt, the right hand consoles it because the pain is our own. This is how it is with compassion.

Once a disciple asked his *guru*, "What is real compassion?" The *guru* took him to a street near the *ashram*. There, he asked the disciple to observe a beggar. A few moments later, an old lady put a coin in his begging bowl. After a while, a wealthy person gave him a 50-rupee note. Then a little boy walked by. He smiled lovingly at the beggar. He went near him and started talking to him, respectfully, as if speaking with an elder sibling. The beggar was very happy. The *guru* asked the disciple, "Of all these three people, who had true compassion?"

The disciple answered, "The rich man."

The *guru* smiled and said, "No, he had neither compassion nor sympathy. His only intention was to show off his philanthropic nature."

"The old lady?" guessed the disciple.

"No," said the *guru*. "The old lady had sympathy, but she did not see the beggar as her own. She did not really want to remove his poverty. We can only call the child's attitude true compassion. He treated the beggar as if he were his own. Though the boy could not help the beggar in any significant way, there was a heart connection and mutual understanding. What the boy showed the beggar was true compassion."

The world does not need our fleeting sympathy; it needs our heartfelt compassion. Compassion rises when we feel others' happiness and sorrow as our own. Then, there is love and a willingness to serve. Compassion—this is the only medicine that heals wounds of the world.

The Correct Attitude Is Everything

Children, many people live in total disappointment due to problems arising from work and life in general. This is mainly due to their mental attitude or their incorrect outlook on life. Their lives would be greatly transformed if someone could show them the right path and encourage them along it. Then they would no longer feel burdened and could even become positive role models for others.

Once, a college student really wanted to become a doctor. However, he failed the MBBS entrance exam by one mark and was denied admission. Greatly disappointed, his mind did not allow him to join any other course of study. After a while, he gave in to his relatives' desires and applied for a job in a bank. He got the job, but continued to brood over how he had failed to become a doctor. Because of this, he was unable to serve the bank's customers with love or even to smile at them. Realising his mental state, a friend took him to see a *guru*. The man opened up to the *guru* and shared his heart. "My mind is not in my control. I get angry over small things. I don't treat the bank customers with respect. Under these circumstances, I don't think I can continue to work there. What should I do?"

The *guru* comforted him and said, "Son, if I were to send a very close friend there, how would you treat him?"

"I would happily help him with whatever he needed."

"If that is the case, then from now on, look upon each customer as someone specially sent to you by God. Then you will be able to interact with each individual with love."

From that day onwards, the young man experienced a major transformation in his attitude. This transformation reflected in his every thought and action. As he learned to look at each customer as sent by God—as the very image of God—his actions verily became a form of worship. All grief was lifted from his mind. His heart was filled with contentment and satisfaction. He was able to spread the happiness he felt to everyone.

To cultivate the right mental attitude, devotion is very helpful. A person with faith in God will have God as the very centre of his existence. He will see God in everything. He will surrender all his actions to God. Thus, if one can see his actions as worship of God, it not only helps him, but also all of society.

The Path to Peace

Children, when Amma looks at the world today, she feels a lot of sorrow. Everywhere, there are images of tears and bloodshed. People are unable to show compassion even to children. So many innocent lives are sacrificed in wars and terrorist attacks every day. It's true that wars were fought in olden days as well, but back then, one would never fight against someone who was unarmed. Fighting after sunset was also not allowed. Back then, such codes of conduct were followed. Today, however, every method of destruction is acceptable—no matter how cruel or against *dharma*. When we look around, we see a world ruled by the selfish and the egomaniacal.

The root cause of all destruction is ego. Two types of ego are the most destructive. One is the ego of power and wealth. The other is the ego of "Only my view is right! I will not tolerate anything else." Such egoism makes peace and contentment impossible, both in our personal lives and in society as whole.

All viewpoints have their value. We must put in effort to recognise and accept them. We must consciously try to understand everyone's ideas. If we can do so, we can put an end to the pointless war and bloodshed we are seeing around us.

To truly understand and respect the views of others, we must first cultivate love within us. Many people make a lot of effort to learn another language. They have a lot of interest and enthusiasm to do so. However, learning the language of another people is not enough to understand them. For that, we require the language of love—a language we have completely forgotten.

Once, in order to try to raise money for a humanitarian organisation, a group of its volunteers went to speak with the owner of a big business. They described at length the pathetic conditions of the suffering people they were trying to help. Their stories of pain and sadness were enough to make anyone's heart melt, but that businessman was totally unaffected and not at all interested. Full of disappointment, the volunteers prepared to leave. Just then, the businessman said, "Stop. I will ask you a question. If you answer correctly, I will help you. One of my eyes is artificial. Can you tell which one?"

The volunteers looked into his eyes carefully. Then, one of them said, "It's the left eye."

The businessman said, "Amazing! No one has ever been able to tell the difference before. It was very expensive. How were you able to tell?"

The volunteer said, "I looked carefully into both your eyes. The right one showed a tiny bit of compassion. The left one was like a stone. So, I immediately knew that your right eye was the real one."

This businessman is the perfect symbol of today's age. Today, our heads are hot and are hearts are cold. What is needed is the opposite: Our heads should be cool and our hearts should be warm. The cold selfishness in our heart needs to transform into the warmth of love and compassion, and the hot-headedness of ego must transform into the cool, expansiveness of Self-knowledge.

Love and compassion are our greatest wealth. Today we have lost them. Without love and compassion, there is no hope for us or for the world. Let us awaken the softness and tenderness of these divine qualities within our heart.

Keep the Attitude of a Beginner

Children, we must always maintain the attitude of a beginner. Having this attitude means to have humility, optimistic faith and enthusiasm. For this, we need the open-heartedness to accept all good things, no matter from where they come. If we can do this, then humility, optimistic faith and enthusiasm will automatically waken within us. Then we will be able to learn from all our experiences. We will also react correctly in all circumstances. On the other hand, if our heart is not open, not only will we fall slave to our ego and stubbornness, but we will also make many mistakes and lose the ability to absorb what is good for us. Such an attitude leads to self-destruction.

One day during the Mahabharata War, Arjuna and Karna faced each other in battle. Lord Krishna was driving the chariot for Arjuna. Salya was the charioteer for Karna. Arjuna and Karna showered each other with arrows. Finally, with the intention of bringing down Arjuna, Karna prepared to shoot an arrow at Arjuna's head. Seeing this, Salya said, "Karna, if you want to kill Arjuna, don't aim at his head. Aim at his neck."

Karna egoistically replied, "Once I aim, I never change my mind. I will fire this arrow straight towards Arjuna's head!" Karna proceeded to fire the arrow.

Lord Krishna saw the arrow coming straight at Arjuna's head and quickly pushed the chariot down towards the earth with his holy feet. The wheels of the chariot sunk into the earth, and the arrow—which would have hit Arjuna's head—struck only his crown. The crown was hit, but Arjuna was saved. Soon after that, Arjuna killed Karna.

If only Karna had obeyed Salya, he would have hit Arjuna and killed him. But Karna's ego did not allow him to accept Salya's advice. That caused Karna's destruction.

The attitude "I know everything" blocks us from learning. When a cup is full to the brim, what can be added to it? Only when the bucket is empty and sinks into the water can it be filled. Even a Nobel Laureate, if he wants to learn to play the flute, must adopt the attitude of a beginner and become a student under a teacher.

Having the attitude of a beginner is the passage to a world of knowledge and expansiveness. That is the attitude of "I know nothing; please teach me." From that, we will receive grace from everywhere, gain knowledge easily and experience victory in our lives.

www.ingramcontent.com/pod-product-compliance
Lightning Source LLC
LaVergne TN
LVHW051735080426
835511LV00018B/3072